Urban Schools
Designing for high density

RIBA Publishing

© RIBA Publishing, 2020

Published by RIBA Publishing, 66 Portland Place, London, W1B 1NT

ISBN 9781 85946 881 4

The rights of Helen Taylor and Sharon Wright to be identified as the Authors of this Work has been asserted in accordance with the Copyright, Designs and Patents Act 1988 sections 77 and 78.

All rights reserved. No part of this publication may be reproduced, stored in a retrieval system, or transmitted, in any form or by any means, electronic, mechanical, photocopying, recording or otherwise, without prior permission of the copyright owner.

British Library Cataloguing-in-Publication Data
A catalogue record for this book is available from the British Library.

Commissioning Editor: Ginny Mills
Assistant Editor: Clare Holloway
Production: Richard Blackburn
Typeset by Fakenham Prepress Solutions, Norfolk
Printed and bound by Short Run Press Limited, Exeter
Cover images: Front cover and top on back – Ian Bogle Architects. Bottom back cover – Scott Brownrigg

While every effort has been made to check the accuracy and quality of the information given in this publication, neither the Author nor the Publisher accept any responsibility for the subsequent use of this information, for any errors or omissions that it may contain, or for any misunderstandings arising from it.

www.ribapublishing.com

CONTENTS

Foreword	*by Sunand Presad*	iv
Acknowledgements		vi
Editors		vii
Contributors		viii
Introduction	*by Helen Taylor & Dr Sharon Wright*	xiii
Chapter 1	The Dispersed School *by Catherine Burke & Dan Hill*	1
Chapter 2	Education and Global Urbanisation *by Dr Juliet Davis*	11
Chapter 3	Understanding the Urban School *by Gareth Long & Dr Sharon Wright*	21
Chapter 4	Small People, Large Scale: The Early Learning Village, Singapore *by Ian Bogle & Dr Sharon Wright*	33
Chapter 5	Mixed-Use Developments *by Peter Clegg & Dr Joe Jack Williams*	43
Chapter 6	High-Rise Schools *by Helen Taylor*	57
Chapter 7	Reuse, Repurpose, Share *by Michael Buchanan*	71
Chapter 8	The Connected Learner *by Ty Goddard*	85
Chapter 9	The Urban Environment for Learning *by Dianne Western*	93
Chapter 10	Building Schools in Urban Environments *by Helen Taylor*	113
Conclusions	*by Helen Taylor & Dr Sharon Wright*	127
Notes		134
Index		139
Picture Credits		142

FOREWORD

The critique of modernist post-WW2 city planning is now so widely accepted that we see the idea of zoning by use, the design of buildings in isolation from each other and the neglect of context all as things of the past. They have been replaced by a collection of principles that currently go under the catch-all term of 'placemaking'. Curiously, the design of schools – the quintessence of social architecture – has been slower to move on. That is of course a generalisation, and this book richly illustrates the exceptions that open up future possibilities.

Schools built by 19th-century school boards displayed strong urban presence. They were often of three or four storeys, each storey almost twice as high as in later typologies, and generously lit with tall windows. Fitted onto tight sites, some had playgrounds on roofs. After the war such designs were seen simultaneously as both cramped and wasteful. Some of that is understandable: if state education was to be on a par with private education, facilities needed to be as good, and private schools always had, for instance, extensive playing fields. However, when we look back, the Victorian Board School impresses us with its robust materials, thoughtful composition and clever designs, often with an Arts and Crafts sensibility.

In contrast, schools built to official guidance in the 20th century have been almost blind to context. Although some concessions were made as regards the extent of playing fields in central urban locations, the ideal of a two- or maximum three-storey building set in grounds prevailed. The school was a refuge from the city. Pupils might go on trips to museums and theatre but that was the extent of engagement with urban life; they would be taught the skills needed for work, but the setting encountered in workplaces remained remote. The buildings rarely had any urban presence, with the favoured pattern being to set them back from the street, beyond a parking forecourt.

If we are to continue to deliver schools near to where people live, it is inevitable that as urban density goes up there will be pressure on land allocated for a school. High-density schools are not new: cities like New York and Hong Kong have long accommodated schools in high-rise buildings, with field sport often provided for via bus trips. However, there has been a tendency to see this as a compromise. What this book shows is that we can embrace the urban context and seize the possibilities it offers while accommodating the need for physical and outdoor activities in dynamic ways.

New ways of learning, teaching and working – together with better understanding of young people's cognitive and emotional development – have in any case brought new design approaches to schools. If we add to this the parallel explosion of possibilities brought about by digital technology, the impact on school design is huge. A great strength of this book is in showing through case studies and essays how such factors can interact with a more intense relationship between schools and high-density neighbourhoods to create transformational places.

Looking forward, perhaps we will see progressive erasure of the opposition between nature and the city. The best high-density schools may be pioneers in showing what that might be like.

Sunand Prasad PPRIBA
Senior Partner, Penoyre & Prasad

ACKNOWLEDGEMENTS

Our thanks to everyone who has contributed to this book. We know that developing schools for high-density areas is an emerging theme and, as such, requires new ways of thinking about old challenges. We have been grateful for the measured way in which chapter contributors have looked in detail at the pros and cons of high-density schools and their thoughtful contributions on both the educational experience and the quality of the urban landscape.

Thanks to Ginny Mills, Clare Holloway and the team at RIBA Publishing for patiently guiding us through the process of making a book.

A number of professionals shared their experience and expertise to help us develop the themes in the book and we are particularly grateful to Claire Jackson, Marcel Hendricks, Steve Smith, Gill Wynne Williams, Claire Barton, Bryan Schnabel and Inigo Woolf for their input.

We are also grateful to all the practices and individuals who generously allowed us to use photographs, drawings and diagrams of their urban school projects.

A special thanks to the team at Scott Brownrigg and colleagues at the-learning-crowd for their ideas, critique and endless enthusiasm for designing better schools.

EDITORS

Helen Taylor RIBA, Director of Practice, Scott Brownrigg. Helen is a chartered architect and champions inclusive, sustainable education in the profession as well as projects at collaborative international design practice, Scott Brownrigg. Specialising in Education design for nearly 20 years, she recently led a proposal for an innovative multi-storey Academy in the UK. She is passionate about cross industry collaboration, engagement and research and is currently a member of the Board of the RIBA. Helen was a founder member and co-chair of Architects for Change, the RIBA's Equality & Diversity Forum and Convenor of the RIBA Schools Client Forum. She played a significant role in the establishment of Modern Apprenticeships in Architecture.

Dr Sharon Wright, Senior Associate, the-learning-crowd. Sharon specialises in school design and has particular expertise in brief development, options appraisal, stakeholder engagement, and post occupancy evaluation. Over the past 17 years she has worked with education leaders, architects and contractors to create the best possible learning environments on a wide range of projects nationally and internationally. Previously she spent 12 years in the Civil Service working on education and employment policy and was a Fellow in Organisational Development with OPM before becoming Managing Director of the not for profit company School Works. Sharon is a Doctor in Education from King's College London. She is a Fellow of the RSA, a Fellow of the British American Project, a Member of the RIBA Validation Panel, and is on the Advisory Board of the Young Dancers Academy in West London.

CONTRIBUTORS

Ian Bogle, Founder, Bogle Architects. Ian founded Bogle Architects in 2012 and the award winning practice is now active in countries within South America, Asia, Africa, Europe and the UK across several building typologies and sectors. Ian believes in education through encouragement and opportunity, is also a Trustee of the Jubilee Gardens Trust, and is frequently invited to lecture on Architecture, Urban and Environmental Design across the international conference circuit.

Michael Buchanan, Education Consultant. Michael has extensive experience in education and school design, latterly as Education Director leading the sector strategy at construction company Galliford Try, where he led the innovation of the multi-award winning 'Optimum Schools' approach to design and construction efficiency. Prior to that, he was Education Director at Partnerships for Schools and at consultants Place Group, Expert Adviser to the Design Council's Learning Environments Campaign, a secondary head teacher, Local Authority Senior Adviser, Ofsted Registered Inspector and Lecturer at the University of London.

Catherine Burke, Professor of History of Education at the Faculty of Education, University of Cambridge. Catherine is a historian of education whose research focuses on 20th and 21st century progressive education with a particular interest in material contexts. She collaborates with architects designing schools today who are interested in drawing useful knowledge from past efforts to design schools to fit the child. She is currently working on transatlantic transferences of knowledge about the design of education during the 'open learning' era of the 1960s and 70s.

CONTRIBUTORS IX

Prof Peter Clegg, Senior Partner, Feilden Clegg Bradley Studios.
Peter is a Professor of Architecture at the University of Bath and a founding partner of Feilden Clegg Bradley Studios who over the last 20 years have designed multi-award winning secondary schools often in very constrained urban sites. He recently wrote 'Learning from Schools', a reflective history of the practice's involvement with the design of spaces for education

Dr Juliet Davis, Reader in Architecture and Urbanism at Cardiff University.
Juliet is a Reader in Architecture and Urbanism at the Welsh School of Architecture at Cardiff University. She is Director of the Postgraduate Taught Programmes and teaches on the Masters in Urban Design. Her research interests include regeneration, urban inclusion, resilience and futures. Her AHRC-funded PhD, completed at the London School of Economics' Cities Programme in 2011, explored the planning and urban design of London's 2012 Olympic urban legacy, focussing on regeneration concepts, strategies and issues. She initially trained as an architect, graduating from Cambridge University with a first-class degree in 1995, and practiced as an architect for ten years in London before entering academia in 2007.

Ty Goddard, Co-founder of The Education Foundation and Chair of Edtech. Ty is a leading expert on education reform and has worked as an adviser to the Department for Education on Extended Schools, was Founder and Director of the British Council for School Environments, Managing Director of the award winning design company School Work, and Strategic Community Manager at Brighton and Hove City Council. He was also elected Chair of Education in Lambeth.

Dan Hill, Director of Strategic Design at Vinnova, the Swedish government's innovation agency. A designer and urbanist, Dan's previous leadership positions have included Arup, Future Cities Catapult, Fabrica, SITRA and BBC. He is a visiting professor at UCL Bartlett School of Architecture in London and an adjunct professor at RMIT University in Melbourne, and is one of the Mayor of London's Design Advocates.

Gareth Long, Director, the-learning-crowd. Gareth is a former secondary head teacher and has been advising on the design of new schools, especially in developing education design briefs, for many years throughout the UK and also internationally. He formed the-learning-crowd several years ago and works with schools, architects, contractors, local authorities and governments.

CONTRIBUTORS   XI

Dianne Western, Director, The Landscape Partnership. Dianne is a Chartered Landscape Architect with over 32 years' experience in environmental planning and landscape and urban design. Over the last 20 years she has worked extensively in the education sector, site planning and designing the outdoor environment for schools under PFI, BSF, Academy and EFSA Framework programmes as well as traditional procurement routes.

Dr Joe Jack Williams, Researcher, Feilden Clegg Bradley Studios. Following a period of working as a consultant engineer, Joe undertook a doctorate to understand the impact of new school buildings on the occupants. He now works within FCBStudios, feeding back lessons from POEs into future projects, as well as the current secretary for the CIBSE School Design group.

INTRODUCTION

Helen Taylor & Dr Sharon Wright

Our cities are facing challenges in how they accommodate an increasing population. More school places are needed than ever before but land is in short supply and funding is limited. In this book we look at how the city can continue to provide the best education experience for children when space is tight.

As a sector we are working hard to deliver more for less. This includes making the most of smaller sites through creative design, and finding new ways to build schools using cost-effective materials and modern methods of construction. We are not suggesting that these new high density approaches are easy options – indeed, in many cases they would not be the preferred choice of how to accommodate school places. However, with careful planning and innovative use of existing and new buildings and external landscape, they can provide excellent spaces for high-quality education.

We asked the chapter authors to look at a series of themes including how we view the issues of delivering education within the city. We were mindful that external landscape is a vital part of every child's educational experience and a particular challenge within the urban context. If we think of a school as simply a building we are missing an opportunity to challenge our conception of where and how young people are educated. The dispersed school, using a variety of sites and technology to support learning, is one emerging model. We also wanted to look at how we are creating and using educational buildings, so have explored tall schools, mixed-use developments and adaptive reuse of existing buildings.

We have used case studies from around the world and referenced historic examples in order to explore the educational, architectural, planning, construction and regulatory context that is driving this new wave of school designs.

Drawing on contributions from across disciplines, each of our authors looked at the issues from a different perspective.

Our first two contributions set the scene by considering how children experience the city, and in particular education, within their urban area. In **Chapter 1**, Catherine Burke and Dan Hill consider whether reimagining 'the city as a school' in the design of urban education might help us to explore the possibilities of how we deliver in the urban context. (This is further considered in Chapter 8, which looks specifically at Espoo in Finland where this idea has been brought to life.) In **Chapter 2**, Juliet Davis argues that, although a global priority, the provision of educational infrastructure in disadvantaged urban areas continues to be a challenge. There are emerging examples of how this issue is being tackled and they bring learning for both developing and developed countries. Both authors explore how schools can become more integrated and inclusive in the urban setting.

In **Chapter 3**, Gareth Long and Sharon Wright argue that, in order to design high quality urban schools that meet a whole range of educational needs, the educator and architect must work together. In particular, school leaders can be pragmatic in how they address the challenges of high-density schools, considering new curriculum delivery and school organisational solutions through the design process.

By way of an extended case study to illustrate the points in Chapter 3, Ian Bogle and Sharon Wright use **Chapter 4** to interrogate our perceptions about early years education spaces. The Early Learning Village (ELV) in Singapore, which opened in August 2017, set out to do this on a larger scale than anything we have seen previously. Exploring the rationale and design concept of this unique environment provides lessons as to how we might challenge our thinking for the future.

The next two chapters explore the two main models of new-build, high-density schools that are starting to emerge across the world. In **Chapter 5**, Peter Clegg and Joe Jack Williams review the principles and rationale for well-designed mixed-use developments where schools share spaces with some combination of housing, commercial or other public services delivery. As mixed-use developments become an increasingly prevalent way to maximise available land and budgets, this chapter looks at both the very good reasons to build mixed-use developments and some of the key pitfalls to avoid. In **Chapter 6**, Helen Taylor looks at high-rise schools in the UK and around the world. Although high-rise schools are a relatively new concept, educationalists and architects are having to work closely together to develop imaginative and visionary solutions that not only work as positive, flexible learning spaces but also still create a sense of community within the school and a positive relationship with the surrounding urban fabric and the natural world.

Many buildings are currently being repurposed for educational use and in **Chapter 7**, Michael Buchanan examines how existing redundant or underused buildings are being adaptively reused and repurposed to deliver more with what we currently have. Using case studies, he looks at some interesting and high-quality results, as well as highlighting some significant challenges.

Chapter 8 and **Chapter 9** deal with the cross-cutting themes of Information and Communications Technology and access to the external environment for social and educational use. These are major issues when considering the possibilities of high-density schools and the day-to-day experiences of the young people who use them. Digital infrastructure will become increasingly important in how new models of education will be delivered in the future. In Chapter 8 Ty Goddard looks specifically at how technology might help support high-density schools, ensuring students not only have access to high-quality learning but are prepared for their transition to further and higher education and the world of work.

One of the criticisms often levelled at high-density schools is the lack of external space. Traditionally we rely on schools in cities to play a key role in providing the opportunity for time outdoors and contact with the natural world. In Chapter 9, Dianne Western explores the relationship between high-density schools

INTRODUCTION   XV

Figure 0.01 A child's view through a skyscraper's window and glass floor

and private and public open spaces, and whether there are particular challenges in continuing to ensure children benefit from the physical and mental wellbeing of having significant dedicated external learning, play and social space on site.

In **Chapter 10**, Helen Taylor goes on to explore the challenges of building and operating these new models of schools on tight urban sites. Funding, legislative requirements (including planning approvals) and construction challenges all make these sites unique. If it is likely that we will see more of this type of building in our urban areas, policymakers and funders will have to understand where the system needs to change to accommodate this sort of innovation.

Ultimately, we wanted to identify the successes and help the education design world learn the key lessons from them to deliver new solutions which meet the needs of children now and in the future. In doing so we have identified, in our conclusion to the book, the opportunities and challenges for integration of new types of schools into the city. We hope this book will be useful to educators, designers, property developers, constructors, planners and policymakers as they look for new ways to tackle the challenges ahead.

CHAPTER ONE

THE DISPERSED SCHOOL

Catherine Burke & Dan Hill

INTRODUCTION

The streets of our cities are believed to be ever more hostile and dangerous places for children and young people to navigate, whilst images of education in the public mind continue to be restricted to school interiors. But in an era when children have taken it upon themselves to leave the classroom in order to protest and take action on climate change,[1] shouldn't we be conceiving the whole city as an educational environment?

THE CHILD IN THE CITY

In 1978, when Colin Ward embarked on his study of *The Child in the City*,[2] the well-rehearsed Victorian maxim 'children should be seen and not heard' was still generally regarded to be true. Ward was also co-author, with Anthony Fyson, of the earlier *Streetwork: The Exploding School* (1973),[3] published as Ward and Fyson took up their roles as newly appointed education officers for the Town and Country Planning Authority. *Streetwork* imagined the disappearance of any recognisable 'school', as it had become established as a specific place and idea. 'School' would instead by replaced by a system of urban pedagogy whereby children learned – mostly outside the walls of a school building – to question their environment, identify problems and assist in designing solutions. This was considered to be working with the grain of human nature, assisted by children's natural curiosity and the need for them to develop awareness of their self-worth. In *Streetwork*, and in an extensive series of bulletins designed for teachers in schools – the Bulletin for Environmental Education (BEE) – Ward and others advanced the idea of the city as school. This was a radical approach that set out how learning might take place through engagement with pressing problems in environments that were familiar to young people and about which they cared. It belonged to a climate of opinion held by progressive practitioners – architects,

URBAN SCHOOLS: DESIGNING FOR HIGH DENSITY

Figure 1.01 Children playing by the lake at Thamesmead, Greenwich, London, 1970

planners and educationalists – who believed it inevitable that

> schools themselves will move closer to the world … the interpenetration of school and neighbourhood will be promoted by buildings in which design will become ever more open … the classroom 'box' will disappear … the school building will come to be thought of as a social centre…[4]

During the late 1960s, across the Atlantic, a similar projection was voiced and visualised by architects and educators who together could not imagine that the traditional form of schooling as it had developed in the industrial nations could survive a contemporary climate which subjected all modern institutions to radical questioning. The architect Shadrach Woods, for example, argued:

> We see the city as the total school, not the school as 'micro-community' … The theatre of our time is in the streets. Education, then, is urbanism. And urbanism is everybody's business, as is education.[5]

In 1960s America, the possibilities of the city in the school were clearly grasped by a child

THE DISPERSED SCHOOL

Figure 1.02 Looking at the city – The view from the High Line, New York

featured in Robert Coles's essay 'Those Places They Call Schools', which appeared in a 1969 special issue of the *Harvard Educational Review* on the theme of architecture and education. Apart from having 'everything' such as a 'movie theatre' and home comforts,

> A good school would have a road going right through it, or under it, and you could see cars and stores and people, and they'd be looking at you and you wouldn't have to take a bus and go way out into nowhere, just because you're going to school … They shouldn't drag us all over the city, just to see some pictures in a museum and places like that. They could have a big room in the school and we could go and look at things all the time if we wanted, not just once a year.[6]

From another point of view, the educational and social critic Ivan Illich argued in 1971 that schooling promoted a dependency which was the opposite of true education. Instead, he proposed the 'deschooling' of society: rather than being confined to a set curriculum and specific building, education might flourish best through the construction of networks of expertise whereby learning would happen

Figure 1.03 Architecture educators Matt+Fiona provide young people with opportunities to build their own learning spaces in the Made in Oakfield project, Hull

through active engagement with those carrying out everyday tasks in the community.[7]

Children and young people who in 2001 contributed their ideas about how 21st-century education should be experienced agreed with Ward and Fyson that the school might move ever closer to the urban environment. From Jonathan, then aged 17:

'
The school I'd like would be one that was open, in all senses of the word … pupils would have freedom to choose lessons they wanted to do … The school would also be much more integrated into the wider community. The notion of writing prize-winning essays on tropical rainforests without taking some action would be seen as strange. Schools would be part of the local and international community and would take part in solving some of its problems.[8]

What are the barriers to implementing these reconfigured, reimagined educational environments? Were 'school' to 'explode' into the community, as Ward and Fyson envisaged, teaching and learning would happen primarily in the streets and neighbourhoods of our towns and cities, using the public facilities that were designed for community use, and perhaps some of the commercial facilities designed to support our economy. This would transform many things. The profession of teaching and the nature of training and development would by necessity be very different. The responsibility of the urban pedagogue would be to seek out opportunities to engage the whole community in projects that could enable young people to work together to help bring about positive change or to develop skills through involvement in initiatives within the local economy. Cities might become less places of consumption and more places of invention and creation. Could a 'learning path' be a physical experience in the city? Fifty years on, is digital technology now facilitating the scenario that Ward and Fyson imagined?

THE IMPACT OF DIGITAL

Digital technology, or 'tech', actually impacts physical space, despite its early perception as 'cyberspace'. It displaces and transforms. It is having an ever more visible impact on the use and availability of space in our cities: entire job types and services – travel agents, department stores – occupy ever dwindling physical space in the heart of cities, partly due

THE DISPERSED SCHOOL

Figure 1.04 Children engaging with the city – UK Youth Strikes 2019

to digital transformation. Systems like Airbnb suggest a fluidity of use of physical space, via digital interfaces. The growth of app-enabled ride-sharing, car-sharing and soon autonomous vehicles all challenge the dominance of the hugely space-hungry private car in our mobility systems and, if handled strategically, could free up vast amounts of parking space and road space for other uses. Amidst all the noise, we should consider that these digital systems often replace, or 'disintermediate', the undifferentiated and generic, rather than the local and distinctive. Perhaps the only things that may be resilient to these global plays are the super-local and community-based: the independently owned store; the old model of the bottega as mini-factory (workshop in the back, shop in the front); or the 'third place' of library, or community centre, or kindergarten, or distinctive café – all of which you might find in a school.

If one of the impacts of digital on our high streets has been to displace space and move retail out, it equally provides quicker and easier ways of filling those same streets. In the recent past, finding a vacant shop and turning it into a kindergarten would require significant time and patience, filling out apparently endless amounts of paperwork, and many administrative dead ends. Yet just as one can find and book a flight and hotel in a few clicks, without the assistance of a travel agent, it is increasingly easy to match demand to supply in terms of space. Projects like Renew Newcastle in Australia – in which otherwise vacant former retail premises were used to meet a demand for cultural spaces and workspaces – have shown how a small amount of digital assistance can support a community-led campaign and lead to a vastly increased and more diverse utilisation of space in what was previously a rapidly deteriorating town centre.[9]

The 'flipped classroom' is a model of schooling where the traditional learning environment is reversed by delivering instructional content, often online, outside the classroom and using the classroom for collaborative activities. In an underoccupied urban environment, could we create the 'flipped school'? A school turned inside-out and dispersed into a city could be made more viable by embedding digital interactions in physical and natural elements. The 'Internet of Things' – the digital augmentation of everyday physical objects such as screens, sensors, devices, clothes, bikes, plants, etc. – can create fluid forms of wayfinding, exploration and discovery; it connects people in public places via social media-like networks, and enables spaces and places, from flower beds to street corners, to possess embedded learning opportunities, allowing them to be accessed in new ways, to be better understood and augmented with interaction.

This more creative approach to tech also has the potential to balance the use of resources – including energy, water and waste – more effectively. The archetypal big school of 2,000 children in one large inflexible building largely unused during the evening and at weekends, with high running costs and large footprint, next to a busy road or transport hub, could be replaced by a collection of more interesting, diverse, adaptable, decentralised modular units selected and operated in response to need, amidst a safer, cleaner, greener urban environment. The architectural visions of some decades ago provide a blueprint which we must critically re-assess for the 21st century – yet perhaps some of their more generative ideas could finally be realised.

THE DISTRIBUTED SCHOOL

This model of schooling challenges existing approaches to safeguarding. A distributed school model is harder to build a wall around;

Figure 1.05 Ericsson Mixed Reality Prototype Johannesburg – learning in the city

however, the expectation of this provision is not universally applied. Cultural expectations and approaches vary worldwide – in some cases, discussion of how to ensure kids can walk to school safely leads to visions of pervasive surveillance or even sensors embedded in schoolchildren themselves. However, in countries like Japan and Finland, with active, safe streets and a strong social fabric, six- and seven-year-olds happily and safely walk themselves home unaccompanied.

This dispersed schooling approach also touches on a broader question regarding the impact of digital technology on education – one faced by universities most keenly. Given that a pupil can now watch lessons online, what is the point of the school building? We should critically assess what can now be done elsewhere, and therefore find more space for those things that only buildings can do. Some universities are actively researching and designing for learning activities that cannot, or *should not*, be replaced by digital: real socialising, not just social media; meeting experts and peers face to face; working in groups together as a physical and located experience; understanding the true context of place by *being there*; providing a richer diversity of experience; and yes, more efficiently utilising valuable space by intensifying activity.

All of these approaches can create a more intensive, diverse and productive campus experience. Melbourne's RMIT University has found a successful model in their Building 80 on Swanston Street, providing a complex series of malleable, adaptable smaller spaces, a range of diverse experiences and a handful of large lecture theatres, ensuring a buzzing hive of activity, with incredibly high utilisation rates as well as strong learning outcomes.

Figure 1.06 Cultural expectations of children – Unaccompanied travel in Tokyo

And Colin Ward's ideas of urban pedagogy have also come to life. Since its launch in 2015, the RIBA National Schools Programme has enabled over 26,000 children and young people to explore and understand their built environment. For teachers, it promotes

Figure 1.07 Learning outside the classroom: RIBA National Schools programme in action

collaborative teaching methods that harness positive risk-taking and encourage seeing the built environment – including the classroom itself – as a third teacher. For architects, it is an opportunity to participate with their communities and to consider, from a new angle, the social role of architecture in relation to their own practice.

Most might agree with the saying 'It takes a village to raise a child' – or perhaps it can be a city raising a child too – yet most countries still appear to have implicitly decided that education is substantially the responsibility of professional teachers in special buildings called schools set apart for learning. However, perhaps technology, if co-opted to a broader social purpose, provides us with an opportunity to stop building 'schools' and to shift our vision as educators, architects and communities towards a scenario where:

> *Schools will no longer be simple destinations in the systems of circulation, holes in the fabric of the public domain, but will form an integral part of those systems and that domain*[10]

This 'exploded', dispersed schooling offers an endorsement of the inclination and ability of children and young people to critique, reimagine and reconstruct their world for themselves, with and for the communities to which they belong. The architect Giancarlo de Carlo appeared to support such a view when he argued that 'education is the result of experience and the wider and more complex the experience, the deeper and more intense the education'.[11]

Digital technology can unlock a more fluid use of space, and a richer and more complex form of teaching and learning. Making it really work for our spaces and places of learning, as well as our towns and cities, could facilitate such a transformation. However, left to its own devices, tech can often be individualising and reductive, rarely achieving a strong public outcome. It will thus require a new form of 'strategic designer' in national and city government, who will be capable of actively framing urban and education questions more holistically; understanding concepts of public value as well as technology, user experience design and systems thinking; facilitating interaction between education professionals, students of all ages, and the wider public and civic society; and stewarding delivery in a more agile, iterative fashion that produces ongoing learning from real-world interactions. That role is beginning to emerge around the world. A truly participative approach to design, coordinated to draw in and work with multiple perspectives, could enable this broader public outcome from technology.

CONCLUSION

If our efforts as architects, educators and planners were focused on building communities and equipping them to raise the next generation, the role of schools might be very different. The focus for education and change would be far wider than any single building or site. The curriculum would be generated by the local environment from simple to ever more complex scales. The school building might act as a hub – a resource centre containing facilities designed to encourage collaboration and teamwork. Its role would be to foster cooperation and the achievement of real and meaningful goals that the wider community could benefit by and celebrate. In such a scenario, our cities would begin to look very different.

CHAPTER TWO
EDUCATION AND GLOBAL URBANISATION

Dr Juliet Davis

INTRODUCTION

The lack of access to educational opportunities is currently most pronounced in regions of rapid urbanisation and in the fastest growing cities. Some of the most pressing challenges for urban planners relate to the provision of schools in the context of worldwide urbanisation.

GLOBAL URBANISATION

Urbanisation denotes the increase in the share of the world's, or any nation's, population living in urban areas. In 1950, 70% of the world's population was rural. By 2050, 70% of that population is anticipated to be urban. Today, partway between these dates, 55% or just over half of the world's human population lives in urban areas.[1] A major shift in global human settlement patterns is occurring.

This shift is recognised as a global phenomenon. However, urbanisation has not been proceeding (and is not anticipated to proceed) at the same rate all over the world. Since 1950 the population of some cities, notably in the Global North, which urbanised in the 19th century, has stagnated and even begun to reduce. The population of others, however, particularly those located in the Global South, has risen exponentially in the same timeframe. Kinshasa and Shenzhen, for example, were both small cities of a few thousand inhabitants in 1950, but now each have populations of around nine million people. Of the 41 cities anticipated to be megacities in 2030, 34 are located in the Global South,[2] and projections suggest that the most extensive and rapid urbanisation will occur in Asia and Africa, particularly Southern Asia and sub-Saharan Africa, over the coming decade. Cities such as Lagos, Dar es Salaam and Kampala, for example, which already encompass large populations of 17.5 million, 5.5 million and 1.3 million respectively, are expected to double in size by 2030. Jakarta is expected to grow so much as to overtake Tokyo

Figure 2.01 Fastest Growing Cities World Map

in 2030 and become the biggest megacity in the world, accommodating an astounding 35.6 million people.

Urbanisation is largely driven by a combination of endogenous urban growth and migration from rural areas to towns and cities, although conflict and ensuing displacement, humanitarian crises and climate change are increasingly seen as contributors.[3] UNICEF estimates that up to 60% of growth is driven by children born in cities.

As a result, high proportions of the populations of rapidly urban areas are children. In Dar es Salaam, for example, 43% of the population is under the age of 20.[4] In Lagos, that figure is 42%; in Mumbai, 31%. With a growing population come requirements for infrastructure, development and services to cater to diverse needs. Many cities, however, especially those in low-income countries, have been and continue to be ill-equipped to deal with the needs of rising populations.

One of the key ways this is reflected is in the increasing proportion of urban populations living in slums, particularly in the most rapidly urbanising regions. Of the world's total urban population, 30% is estimated to live in slums. But in Southern Asia, 31% are slum-dwellers, and the figure rises to a staggering 60% in sub-Saharan Africa. In official parlance, slums are defined according to a range of characteristics which particular urban areas may exhibit to differing degrees. They are typically zones of *substandard housing*, are characterised by *non-compliance with planning and building regulations*, often involve the *informal occupation of land* and lack access to *basic services* (sanitation facilities, clean water sources, waste collection systems, electricity, surfaced roads and footpaths, street lighting and rainwater drainage).[5] Deficiencies in the provision of educational infrastructure are also a feature of cities in low-income regions where urbanisation is characterised by the growth of settlements exhibiting these characteristics.

EDUCATION ON THE AGENDA

Currently, the number of children who are denied access to education worldwide stands at 262 million.[6] A closer look at the geographical distribution of this figure shows that the problem is concentrated in the regions of most rapid urbanisation. Of all children and adolescents in sub-Saharan Africa 31.7% are out of school, as are 22.5% of those in Southern Asia, figures that contrast with the 17.8% of children out of school globally and the 4.3% across Europe and North America (*see* Figure 2.02). Reflecting histories of low educational attainment according to global benchmarks, the lowest adult literacy rates in the world are identified with these areas too. South and West Asia, between them, are home to more than half of the world's illiterate population while 22% of all illiterate adults live in sub-Saharan Africa.

According to UNESCO, the problem is pronounced in rural areas within these regions. Indeed, migrants to cities are often in search of better opportunities, including education. However, many children and adolescents living in slums and informal settlements are shown to actually have less access to education than their rural counterparts and, in consequence, children from poor urban neighbourhoods are recognised as among the least likely to attend school.[7] In other words, these children are not able to benefit from the greater proximity to resources and opportunities that urban density is often said to offer. How, or to what extent, present and rising needs for education infrastructure are addressed will have implications for future patterns of urban inequality, as levels of education and forms of persistent disadvantage are connected.

The significance of this is reflected in the prioritisation of education within international development goals. At the turn of the 21st century, ensuring that all children could 'complete a full course of primary schooling education' was established as the second of the United Nation's (UN) Millennium Development Goals. In September 2015, Goal 4 of the UN's Sustainable Development Goals was defined as being to ensure 'inclusive and equitable quality education and promote lifelong learning opportunities for all'. In 2016, UN Habitat similarly emphasised education in its New Urban Agenda, outlining a vision of future human settlements offering 'equal access for all to public goods and quality services such as food security and nutrition, health, education, infrastructure, mobility and transportation, energy, air quality and livelihoods'.[8]

URBAN SCHOOLS: DESIGNING FOR HIGH DENSITY

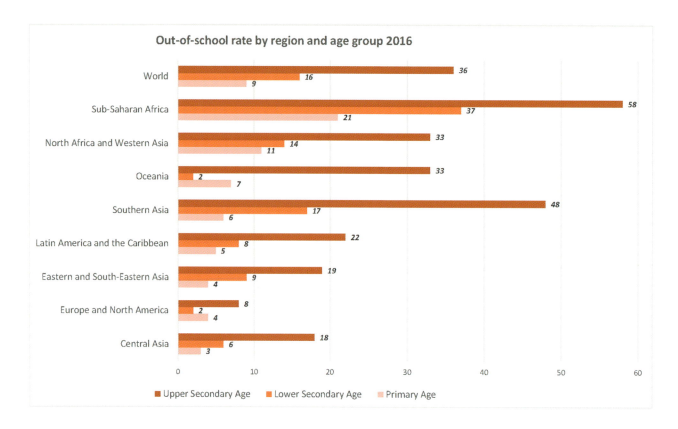

Figure 2.02 Children out of school by region and age group, 2016

While these goals may be framed in terms of global statistics, issues affecting provision and access vary across spatial and social contexts. Collaboration between international, national and local organisations and actors is needed to ensure that global goals translate meaningfully and effectively into specific contexts. Much emphasis is placed on the need for national governments to commit to making education compulsory, financing free education for all, addressing standards of education and attainment and monitoring outcomes. But policies and plans to manage urban growth and ensure access to infrastructure and services are, along with architectural design, also key to addressing barriers to participation in education and creating routes out of urban poverty.

PLANNING AND DESIGN CHALLENGES

Given the anticipated scale of urbanisation, and the current lack of planning capacity and strategy reflected by the spread of slums, there is clearly a pressing need for cities to plan for their urban growth. This, UN Habitat suggests, is not just a matter of projecting the future from past trends, but of developing tools to map and build understandings over time of the complex forces shaping migration patterns, urban growth, changing demographics, and their possible trajectories.[9] Given that uncontrolled urbanisation has often resulted in sprawl and numerous deficits in terms of transport and social infrastructure (including schools), carbon efficiency, services and affordable housing, future strategies for growth must tackle all these issues, but without adopting a proscriptive approach to urban form.[10]

But cities also need to address the legacies of the lack of planning which has resulted in the growth of slums and informal settlements. A major issue affecting the provision of resources and services to existing slums, including educational infrastructure, is the basic lack of visibility that many slums have. Some governments will not provide such resources in settlements regarded as illegal. For schooling, this often leaves families in such settlements reliant on ad hoc systems of private education provision and/or requires children to travel outside their neighbourhoods – important factors seen to shape low levels of attendance among poor urban children.[11] In the context of existing slums, therefore, there continues to be a need for better recognition of slum-dwellers' rights as citizens as a starting point to addressing education issues.

Unfortunately, the desire to simply eradicate slums has persisted in many cities, leading to forced evictions and the breaking of social ties, attachments and even social infrastructures. Notwithstanding, there has been growing recognition worldwide of the benefits of slum upgrade strategies in place of such destructive approaches. These upgrade strategies often entail the legalisation of properties alongside the installation of services and infrastructures within the fabrics of existing developments – though, to benefit existing communities, this must be done in ways that avoid displacing them through formalisation or by facilitating the commodification of property. Schools must routinely be part of these strategies if current barriers to attendance and attainment at all levels of education in poor urban areas are to be addressed.[12]

Upgrading settlements is far from straightforward. As Satterthwaite argues, spatial constraints within slums, particularly high-density ones, mean that introducing infrastructure, public spaces or services usually requires some loss of housing.[13] Spatial thinking and design ingenuity is needed to identify suitable sites and sensitive solutions, as exemplified by the city of Medellín in Colombia where, under the initiative of Mayor Sergio Fajardo (2003–7), slum upgrade strategies have included the introduction of public transport via cable car, allowing the demolition of housing to be minimised. There has also been investment in new education infrastructure such as the Antonio Derka School by Obranegra Arquitectos, situated beside one of the poorest and, historically, most violent 'barrios' of the city.[14] Planning and design processes that enable local communities to define their own needs and requirements are key to ensuring satisfactory outcomes in selecting locations, developing infrastructure and incrementally adapting neighbourhoods.[15]

As UNICEF points out, better access to early years, primary and secondary education is crucial, but so too is access to 'positive, welcoming and safe learning spaces'.[16] This is necessary to overcome cultural and emotional

URBAN SCHOOLS: DESIGNING FOR HIGH DENSITY

barriers to participation in education – including fear of institutions, shame regarding economic status, a sense of alienation and lack of confidence – and to develop a range of capabilities through education.[17] Providing this kind of access is a matter of school culture and teaching practice but it is also a challenge for the design and construction of urban schools.

For the reasons discussed, the need for schools is great within some of the poorest areas of rapidly urbanising cities. Those that exist are typically one-offs. The following examples are indeed highly specific responses to the local environment, yet they all represent attempts to maximise benefits within the context of tight budgets and, as such, offer sources of inspiration for future practice worldwide.

CASE STUDIES

Some of the sprawl of Lagos in recent decades has extended over the very edge of the city's frontier on the Lagos lagoon, producing a makeshift water city. The Makoko Floating School (Figure 2.03), shortlisted for the 2016 Aga Khan Award, was designed by NLÉ

Figure 2.03 NLÉ, Makoko Floating School, Nigeria, 2012

EDUCATION AND GLOBAL URBANISATION 17

Architects in 2012.[18] Developing the programme and structure involved working closely with the local community. The three-storey assemblage comprised a platform supported on a raft of empty barrels, enabling it to float, and a series of parallel timber A-frames containing classrooms and a playground. Rooftop photovoltaic cells collecting solar energy, a water catchment system and natural ventilation addressed issues of lack of services in the settlement, allowing it to be self-sustaining. Lack of maintenance and a storm led to the building's collapse, however, highlighting the need for effective management in the life of social infrastructure beyond design and construction.

Community engagement was also key to the design of the Lycée Schorge Secondary School in the city of Koudougou, Burkina Faso, by Diébédo Francis Kéré, which opened in 2016.[19]

Figure 2.04 Kéré Architecture, Diébédo Francis Kéré, Lycée Schorge Secondary School, 2016

URBAN SCHOOLS: DESIGNING FOR HIGH DENSITY

Burkina Faso is one of the poorest countries in the world, yet one of the most rapidly urbanising. The school is on an open site at the developing edge of the city, enabling the designers to avoid the complexities of building amid existing development while providing a resource that the future population will benefit from. Addressing tough environmental conditions including wind, dust and heat, the building, made up of nine modules including classrooms, offices, library and a dental clinic, forms a carapace around a protected space which is available for use by the entire community. Much thought was given to how architecture made of simply, readily accessible materials could create thermally comfortable space, so aiding the process of learning (see Figure 2.04).

Another example is Anna Heringer's METI (Modern Education and Training Institute) school in Rudrapur, Bangladesh, designed with Eike Roswag.[20] Though Rudrapur is a small place, Bangladesh is among the most densely populated countries on earth and urbanising rapidly. The bamboo- and earth-built architecture expresses an aim to provide alternatives to conventional classroom teaching and through an imaginative sequence of learning spaces. These include three classrooms, an open, multipurpose hall on the first floor and a system of organic 'caves' to which children can retreat to read or gather in small groups (see Figure 2.05).

Figure 2.05 Anna Heringer, METI School, Bangladesh

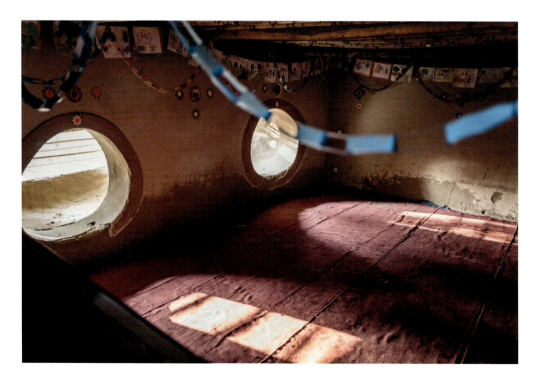

EDUCATION AND GLOBAL URBANISATION

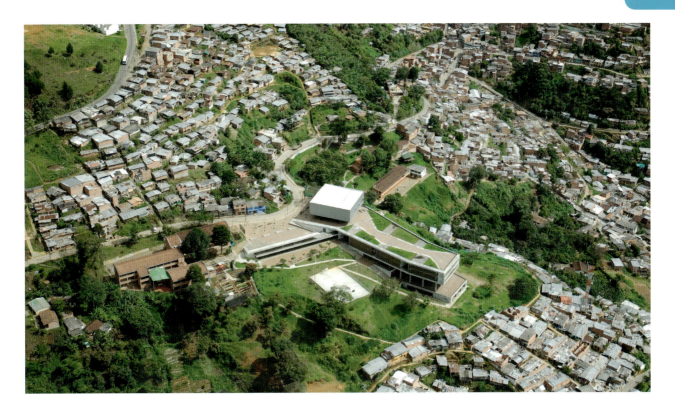

Finally, the Antonio Derka School, also designed by Obranegra Arquitectos, is an example of intervention within a dense existing site, one posing the additional challenge of being steeply sloped. The rectilinear form of the largely masonry building juts out of the slope, offering a social space for local people at roof level and two floors containing classrooms, administrative offices, a lab, cafeteria and day-care centre beneath it (Figure 2.06).

CONCLUSION

These four examples all offer inspiration and hope in the face of the major challenges presented by global issues of inequality and social exclusion in the context of rapid urbanisation. They also illustrate the value that architectural design can bring to processes of addressing them through education. In particular, they demonstrate an imaginative responsiveness to topographical and climatic circumstances that yields comfortable, specific and low-impact architecture. They also show how schools can be far more than generic, mono-functional structures delivered through top-down processes but be attuned to and woven into the social, cultural and material fabrics of local communities.

Figure 2.06 Obranegra Arquitectos, Antonio Derka School, Medellín, Colombia, 2011

CHAPTER THREE

UNDERSTANDING THE URBAN SCHOOL

Gareth Long & Dr Sharon Wright

INTRODUCTION

Our general understanding of a school tends to be linked to a traditional model of a low-rise primary or secondary building with playing space behind a wall or fence. If we are to address the pressures of space in urban schools we need to rethink this concept. Alongside changing structures in education delivery, it is important to understand the school as a 'community of learners' housed within a building. The building, whether high-rise, part of mixed-use developments, situated in an old office block or dispersed more widely through the city, needs to be designed to meet the educational needs of that community and not be dictated solely by the available space. When senior leaders in schools are able to work creatively with their design teams to develop and test new ways of working, it allows them to innovate in curriculum delivery and school organisation to make new spaces work for their community of learners.

UNDERSTANDING EDUCATIONAL COMPLEXITY

As demand for school places continues to fluctuate across the country, we find that new sites are in short supply and many existing schools in our largest cities are already on confined urban sites with limited options to expand. Guidelines for recommended site areas in these urban schools are often unattainable and this is leading local authorities and other school operators to consider increasingly creative solutions for providing good and outstanding learning environments.

There are over 24,000 schools in England, and we must take care to avoid oversimplifying when we talk broadly about how we can best meet their needs. Indeed, the typology of schools has shifted dramatically over the past 20 years. The introduction of the Academy movement and resulting Multi Academy Trusts (MATs) means that families of schools are no longer always geographically based as they previously were when all maintained schools were under local authority control. Some MATs will have clusters of schools in a particular area, but within a town or city there might be a number of school operators, each with its own identity, ethos and educational approach. In addition, the age ranges a school might cater for have changed: for example, there are increasing number of All Age schools taking pupils from age four to eighteen.

Children with Special Educational Needs (SEN) will also be educated in a range of settings depending on their needs and available provision. Special schools, some with residential accommodation, will cater for a variety of physical needs, emotional and behavioural conditions. Many primary and secondary schools may also have inclusive provision for young people with physical and emotional needs either within their mainstream education or in specialist, integrated units. Children with behaviour needs, or those who are temporarily excluded from mainstream education, may be educated in Alternative Provision or Pupil Referral Units.

While it has always been the case that every school is different because of the context, community and needs it caters for, it could be argued that schools are becoming increasingly differentiated. Other developments are influencing school design, including safeguarding requirements and a better understanding of the positive impact of access to outside space on staff and student health and wellbeing and cognitive development.

THE EDUCATIONAL CHALLENGES OF TALL SCHOOLS

While not common in the UK, 'tall schools' are not a new idea. When the Victorians built their Board Schools, many were at least six storeys tall with mezzanine levels and rooftop playgrounds. Where those buildings are still in use as schools, some have been very successfully extended to accommodate growing pupil populations. However, this continued use is not without its problems and demonstrates that the way education delivery has changed over the past 200 years impacts significantly on space requirements.

BREAKING THE MOULD

Many phases of education are incredibly creative in how they use their environment, and this is especially true where space is restricted. School leaders need to bring this pragmatism to the table when they brief for new schools on restricted sites and work with the design team to develop the right buildings for their learning community. Below we have set out some particular considerations where schools could challenge their own assumptions more rigorously. Some design solutions to these educational issues are covered in later chapters of the book.

(a) Early Years
Younger students in Early Years Foundation Stage (EYFS) are normally located on the ground floor for convenience and safety. On purely organisational grounds, the issues focus around pupil arrival and collection, ensuring all safeguarding issues are complied with. Traditionally, parents drop children off directly to staff or to the classroom door to avoid delaying the start of the day and minimising separation issues; this leads to self-contained secure early years facilities being located on the ground

UNDERSTANDING THE URBAN SCHOOL

CASE STUDY: Notre Dame School, London

Notre Dame RC Girls' School in the London Borough of Southwark was founded in 1855. Currently, the school occupies a cramped site in a series of connected buildings from the 19th, 20th and 21st centuries that cover seven floors, including an occupied basement and attic rooms; there are also a variety of mezzanine levels. The school caters for 620 students aged 11 to 16 on a site surrounded by roads and rail tracks, and there is almost no external space. Despite these environmental challenges, the school has been consistently graded 'Outstanding' in every Ofsted inspection.

Contrary to how we would design a new school, spaces at Notre Dame are not distributed to support curriculum delivery. Due to the small floorplate, some core curriculum subjects cannot be placed together to form a suite of complementary rooms, meaning staff and students miss out on potential opportunities to collaborate and share resources.

Students' movement is an issue in any school where sensible subject adjacencies and well-designed corridors allow young people to travel calmly and quickly between classes to avoid loss of learning time. At Notre Dame the main horizontal circulation, via a relatively narrow staircase, is complex with numerous steps into rooms and between buildings, and with few opportunities for passive supervision.

Staff need to be on duty to supervise student movement at key points during lesson changeover and especially at the end of the day.

To make the school more welcoming for the youngest students a recent four-storey extension was built to act as a Year 7 base. Students stay in their own room, with their own desk for many of their subjects, similar to a primary model, and only move into the main school building for specialist lessons (Science, IT, Art, Drama, Music, Design Technology and PE). This allows them to slowly get used to the main building and to moving around with 500 other students, whilst spending the majority of their time in the new block with their own small

Figure 3.01 Cottrell & Vermeulen, Notre Dame School, London, 2013 – Street frontage

CASE STUDY: Notre Dame School, London (CONTINUED)

Figure 3.02 Cottrell & Vermeulen, Notre Dame School, London, 2013 – New roof terrace

overcrowding, and Physical Education and Sports are largely delivered off site in nearby community facilities.

Understanding how Notre Dame provides high-quality education despite the challenges of a tall school that is not built specifically for the modern curriculum allows us to test our understanding of the spaces that work and do not for high-density schools. In a new tall school many of these design issues could be addressed, but there is also much to learn from the way Notre Dame has organised itself to manage the challenges. The school's ability to be flexible and to adapt has been critical – but this takes time, energy and strong leadership.

roof terrace. This dedicated Year 7 building has also been attractive to parents who like the idea of a transition into secondary school life and were previously nervous about their 11-year-olds having to negotiate 7 storeys in a very crowded context.

However, while this has many advantages in terms of minimising movement, a considerable amount of time can still be spent travelling by both staff and students. This is especially true for those moving from the top of the Year 7 building to rooms high in the main building for their next lesson.

As an organisational solution, the school has moved to longer lessons, with the majority being a 'double' lesson where possible, in order to minimise unnecessary movement. However, due to the school's small dining area, a two-shift lunch arrangement reduces some flexibility in timetabling the school's day.

Although there is a lift in the main school and the Year 7 building, the numerous mezzanine levels and the varying heights of the different buildings means that accessibility is a real challenge for students or staff members with mobility issues. Due to the age of the older building, too, there are no refuge spaces for evacuation chairs, so fire escape is a concern as well.

The limited external area at the school consists of a tiny courtyard, a narrow external dining terrace, a small roof first floor terrace for Year 7 and a shared car park (accommodating three cars) and playground. As a result, Year groups are given a specific external space they can use to avoid

Figure 3.03 Cottrell & Vermeulen, Notre Dame School, London, 2013 – Stairs looking out to the city

floor with direct access on arrival. An added advantage is that it usually means that these pupils should have immediate direct access to external learning spaces, facilitating a core part of the EYFS indoor/outdoor curriculum. A ground floor location also gives easy access to Hall and Dining spaces, an advantage since moving the youngest pupils around a school can be a time-consuming task with the pupils being easily distracted and taking time to get organised.

However, it is not impossible to shift thinking. There are examples of younger students being upstairs with learning balconies and terraces providing external spaces. The Early Learning Village in Singapore (see Chapter 4), where the very youngest pupils are located on the eighth floor and all vertical movement is via large lifts, is one model. Fuji Kindergarten by Tezuka Architects gives 600 children aged 2 to 6 a multi-level environment where 'the architecture itself functions as a giant playground'.[1] While regulations in some countries, including in the Middle East, will only permit the youngest pupils on the ground floor, more flexible approaches have been shown to work.

Figure 3.04 Tezuka Architects, Fuji Kindergarten, 2007 – The architecture as a playground

Figure 3.05 Haverstock, Belham Primary School, Southwark – Roof terrace

(b) Primary

It is not unusual for primary classrooms to be located above ground floor, recognising the significant developments in size and independence that take place from the ages of five to eleven. However, whilst infant age pupils do normally have direct access to external learning spaces, there is increasing awareness of the benefits of outside spaces for older students as well. This often presents real challenges for schools on constrained sites: they may have minimal external area in which to deliver social and curriculum activities, or spend a great deal of time getting children through the building and outside at break and lunchtimes. Primary age children spend much of their day in one class base with one teacher where they access a whole range of subjects with occasional timetabled visits to specialist rooms or central resource spaces like multipurpose halls or libraries. Creative solutions with roof spaces and small terraces directly off classrooms can enrich the learning experience. Clear routes through the building and good visual connections with external areas can also support pupil wellbeing. Chapter 9 looks in more detail at how external spaces can be optimised on tight sites to provide a range of learning opportunities.

(c) Secondary

Every secondary school requires a different mix of spaces to meet its curriculum requirements, particularly if the school has specialisms, vocational courses or an emphasis on certain subjects at Sixth Form. There is no such thing as a 'standard school' as the balance of general and specialist spaces will differ. Schools will also want subject adjacencies to

UNDERSTANDING THE URBAN SCHOOL   27

Figure 3.06 Jestico + Whiles, Cardinal Pole Catholic School, Hackney, 2013 – Central circulation street

Figure 3.07 Walters & Cohen, Regent High School, London, 2014 – 'The Arcade' circulation at the heart of the school

support their Faculty or Departmental model and to encourage cross-curricular learning and co-location of subject specialist staff. This can make designing tall schools a particular challenge as smaller floorplates over a greater number of levels will reduce the flexibility to meet organisational needs.

Managing circulation – especially vertical movement, which is disruptive as it takes time and can provide challenges for supervision – is also an issue in tall schools. One option is for schools to fundamentally rethink the nature of the school day, questioning assumptions around why hundreds of students move endlessly from one general classroom to another six, seven or even eight times a day. They may consider changing the times at which younger and older students start and finish school so that all students are not in the building at the same time. Chapter 6 brings forward examples of how good design can overcome some of these organisational challenges.

(d) Special Educational Needs

The key message about creating a school for pupils with SEN is that there can rarely, if ever, be a generic solution. Whilst there may be similarities in design elements, every special school caters for students with a wide range of individual challenges and difficulties.

The priority for these schools is a design that provides for the pupils' wellbeing and the quality of their day-to-day learning and social experience. Often in designing special schools the main focus is rightly on the needs of the student, ensuring appropriate learning facilities and providing specialist support facilities to meet their individual needs. It is important that staff wellbeing is also fully recognised; working in these schools can be very intense and there are times when staff members need some alone space or opportunities for quiet time.

The Livity School is a primary school in Streatham for children with severe learning difficulties, Profound and Multiple Learning Disabilities (PMLD), Autistic Spectrum Disorder (ASD), and complex medical needs. The school worked closely with Haverstock Architects over a long period to create a learning environment over three floors, challenging the conventional thinking that special schools should be on one or, at most,

Figures 3.08 and 3.09
Haverstock, Livity School, Streatham, 2013 – Play terraces

two levels. Breaking away from tradition, the early years students are based totally on the second floor with their own external play terraces. All parts of the school are accessed via a ramp that winds round the 'heart of the school': this is not just a functional route, but a core design feature that offers 360-degree views of key areas and enables the children to be fully integrated into all aspects of school life. There are sensory elements around the ramp so pupils can learn on the go, whether they are in wheelchairs or walking to different locations.

Learning environments for these students need to be particularly carefully crafted in order to achieve optimal space and light and an appropriately stimulating environment. All surfaces matter and impact the students – walls, floors and ceilings. External space is equally deserving of careful design to provide holistic learning opportunities. There is no reason why a tall building cannot provide a high-quality learning environment for students with a wide variety of needs, as long as there is a clear input from the school to ensure that every element of design is appropriate and adapted to cater to the specific needs of the students.

(e) All Age Schools

All Age schools, with children aged from four to eighteen years old in one building, are becoming increasingly common. These schools not only meet demand for places but also support a smoother transition through the educational phases. They can also be more efficient than building separate Primary and Secondary buildings – for example, reducing the area needed for kitchens and plant

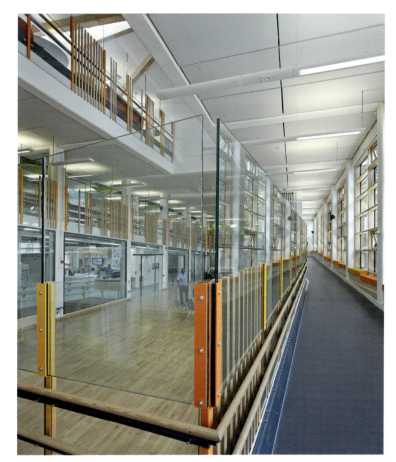

Figure 3.10 Haverstock, Livity School, Streatham, 2013 – The access ramp is placed at the heart of the school

rooms. They need to be carefully planned and there are inevitable issues with timetabling shared spaces and the need to ensure age-appropriate learning spaces and furniture solutions, but they offer the ability to deliver an enriched curriculum for the younger years and greater staff development by teaching across phases.

Figure 3.11

van Heyningen and Haward, St Benedict School, Ealing, 2017 – An all-age school

In designing these schools it is important to ensure that pupils will have access to specialist staff and specialist facilities from a young age and that staff can link work across Key Stages, sharing knowledge and expertise for consistency in teaching and assessment strategies, and can develop a pastoral system that caters for the needs of each student at each stage of their learning. On restricted sites this cross-phase working can present real challenges in getting the right space adjacencies.

Parents also often need to be reassured about the approach to safety and safeguarding issues, how the different phases will be organised and managed, and how the building will operate in practice to cater for such a wide age range. As a relatively new model of schooling, there are not large numbers of All Age schools in the UK to draw on currently, but we would suggest that this is an area for further research in the future.

CONCLUSION

In many ways the process of designing high-density schools is no different to designing schools on large open sites. Understanding the school vision, ethos and curriculum requirements and the social needs of the school community is key. What is different about high-density schools is the need to challenge assumptions about educational delivery. If the building is significantly different then it is likely the school will need to operate in different ways.

Encouraging the school client to explore options for the curriculum and school day, modelling how spaces will be managed and students will flow around the building, developing visuals to allow parents to feel confident, are all key. This doesn't necessarily mean additional cost, but it does require additional time at the design stage for discussion and testing ideas.

CHAPTER FOUR

SMALL PEOPLE, LARGE SCALE

The Early Learning Village, Singapore

Ian Bogle & Dr Sharon Wright

INTRODUCTION

When we think of early years settings we tend to think of domestic-scale nurseries and schools. Yet there is no reason why, when space is limited, we cannot still create a homely, age-appropriate learning environment for the youngest children within a high-density building. Whether sharing space with other educational facilities, housing or community spaces, Early Learning has traditionally been on the ground floor, small in scale, and largely segregated to allow good parental access and ensure safeguarding. This extended case study allows us to explore how creative design solutions and innovative educational thinking can change the way we think about what is possible.

THE EARLY LEARNING VILLAGE, SINGAPORE

The Early Learning Village (ELV), Singapore, which opened in August 2017, set out to do this on a larger scale than anything we have seen in the UK. Exploring the rationale and design concept for this school provides lessons as to how we might challenge our thinking for the future.

Bogle Architects were approached by global schools operator Cognita to create a world first in early years education – a facility for over 2,100 children aged 18 months to 5 years old and 350 staff in Singapore. The initial meeting to discuss the client brief was held in Zürich the day before Christmas 2013, sending the design team off on the festive break to think through the scale and challenges presented by the brief. The client, Cognita Asia, already operated two schools in Singapore: the Australian International School (AIS) and the Stamford American International School (SAIS). This new facility was to be an extension to the existing AIS but would provide early years education for both schools on the same campus.

Cognita's brief stipulated that the project should be a model for future schools of

URBAN SCHOOLS: DESIGNING FOR HIGH DENSITY

this nature, providing facilities rarely seen in pre-school buildings, including external discovery play zones, a swimming pool, a flexible multipurpose hall and specialist subject classes for art, music and dance. The key challenges were to ensure that the significant volume was not intimidating for small children and that circulation worked well given the scale of the school, and to design a building that was essentially playful and fun as well as flexible enough to accommodate changing market conditions.

Bogle Architects looked for similar scale facilities around the world but the largest early years facility they identified was for 600 children in a bespoke school in Tokyo, Japan. They recognised the scale of the challenge but were excited by the possibilities and in January 2014 embarked on the journey to design the ELV. Their experience in designing education facilities was challenged immediately by understanding the nature of the occupiers – small children – some of whom would not yet be at walking stage in their personal development. A whole host of concerns quickly arose around noise, wayfinding, traffic, safeguarding, arrivals and departures, fire safety and evacuation, among others. Quickly realising this was no ordinary building, the design team went through each constraint in a logical fashion, seeing the project as an opportunity to test and question the norm.

To cater for the number of children on site, the entire ground floor was to be occupied by two separate drop-off/pick-up areas for each school, and for bus, motorcycle and car parking. How then do you manoeuvre 2,100 children, some of whom are not yet walking, into and out of a building over a 30-minute period at the start and end of the school day? The solution was to minimise movement so that the youngest and

Figure 4.01 Bogle Architects, ELV, Singapore, 2017 – Cross-section

SMALL PEOPLE, LARGE SCALE   35

Key for Figure 4.01 and 4.02
1. Classroom
2. External Play Area
3. Internal Play Area
4. Teaching Kitchen
5. Admissions
6. Swimming Pool
7. Multi Purpose Hall
8. Admin Offices

least ambulant would be moved only once a day. The rest of the time they would be in their dedicated learning area, scrambling around on the floor. This decision led to placing, somewhat counterintuitively, the youngest children on Level 8, the top floor. As a result, the older, more ambulant children use the stairs to get to their classrooms on the first floor. This provides them with a degree of autonomy and progression, preparing the children for the next phase of their educational journey.

With the intermediate years distributed

Figure 4.02 Bogle Architects, ELV, Singapore, 2017 – Level 2 plan

between Levels 2 and 7, the issue became one of minimising congestion of this vertical distribution of hundreds of children requiring varying degrees of supervision. Bogle Architects devised a highly regimented solution by creating 'mustering points'. Taking advantage of the taller floor-to-floor height on the ground floor (to allow for vehicle distribution), they located a mezzanine floor between the ground and first floors to create mustering areas which serve as a holding location for the children at the beginning and end of the school day. Here children can be dropped off, collected and taken to their respective classes. This strategy minimised the number of lift trips by moving larger groups of 15 to 20 children at one time (rather than smaller groups of one or two as they arrive). To make these mustering areas useful throughout the remainder of the day, they are also used as specialist teaching classrooms incorporating Music, Art and some playful Science.

From the muster points the children then proceed to their learning 'cluster' – a sequence of four self-contained classrooms effectively mimicking a typical nursery 'at the end of the road'. The four classrooms are interlinked both through the circulation space and between classrooms and external balconies. They are designed as such so that different pedagogies can be incorporated by the teaching staff, allowing for individual closed classrooms or more open and interlinked team teaching and collaboration. In addition, they enable free-flowing indoor/outdoor curriculum delivery.

The clusters also contain the central 'peanut' spaces which incorporate the varying age-appropriate WC provision, staff rooms and the teaching kitchens. The peanut shape is a direct response to the curvilinear circulation philosophy – minimising sharp corners, where possible, to allow for free-flowing movement but also providing clearer sight lines to minimise 'bumping into' accidents.

Part of the client's Reggio Emilia learning philosophy was the desire for every classroom to have its own dedicated external play space. This was a challenge not just because of the hot and humid Singaporean environment but also because none of the learning spaces was on the ground floor (as would be the case in a traditional early years setting).

To accommodate the client's brief, balconies project off each classroom at the upper levels. This arrangement means that the balcony above one classroom partially shades and protects the external space below, creating a cantilevered architecture that performs a practical physical function but also gives a playful effect on the exterior of the building.

To break the scale of the building there are 28 clusters stacked atop one another, creating an 8-storey building at the peak. However, they are intentionally stacked towards the rear of the site to create a visual perspective and ensure the building feels lower towards the arrival point, playing with the art of the picturesque.

Canopies of different sizes project from the stacked clusters at varying heights. Primarily designed as weather protection from Singapore's intense sun and torrential rain, these also add to the picturesque visual play that greets students and staff on arrival. These canopies cover the external play spaces which are primarily used by the older children, providing ball game areas, run-around space and external gardening spaces where food is grown as part of the learning experience.

Child safeguarding was a key issue for the client and design team, particularly as the

SMALL PEOPLE, LARGE SCALE

Figure 4.03 Bogle Architects, ELV, Singapore, 2017 – Projecting balconies

entire school is elevated above ground. To meet concerns, the edges of all externally accessible areas are protected by a variety of vertical balustrades. The main external play spaces feature a metre-wide landscape buffer between the edge of the building and the 2m-high balustrades, while the classroom external spaces are also surrounded with a 2m glass balustrade with some low-level manifestation so the children cannot look directly downwards. These spaces are also constantly supervised by one teacher and two assistants per classroom.

The client brief also stipulated an age-neutral exterior with an age-appropriate interior. The main classrooms are clad with a Glassfibre Reinforced Concrete (GRC) rain-screen interspersed with horizontal windows at varying heights. Copings are inclined back towards the building to allow for standing water to go behind the screen, minimising the amount of visual streaking – a real problem in the Singaporean climate.

The challenge here was not to celebrate the scale but instead to make the building feel small, curious and playful, just like its occupants.

38 URBAN SCHOOLS: DESIGNING FOR HIGH DENSITY

Figure 4.04 Bogle Architects, ELV, Singapore, 2017 – Typical cluster

To achieve this, the design team created a wealth of exciting and intriguing spaces. They also provided low-level windows with window seats, allowing the children to watch what is going on outside, and apparently these have become the most popular places to sit in the classrooms.

This complex project has been a challenging exercise in terms of connectivity and vertical transportation to ensure that significant numbers of adults and children can orientate themselves easily around the building. The result is a building that feels both intimate and personalised, visually complex yet legible, and provides a rich learning environment for pupils, parents, and staff.

DOES IT WORK?

Building users certainly think so. Chris Jansen, CEO of Cognita, understands the benefit of well-designed early years environments: the highest quality experience at the earliest stages of learning, he says, will reap benefits at every step of a child's subsequent educational journey, and beyond. An essential aspect of that experience is the educational environment itself. Jansen sees the Early Learning Village as

SMALL PEOPLE, LARGE SCALE

Figure 4.05 Bogle Architects, ELV, Singapore, 2017 – ETFE Conopies

an unparalleled project, both innovative and inspiring – a breath-taking design that is at all times centred on the child and the exploration and discovery they need to flourish.[1] It reflects Cognita's conviction that early years education is the all-important foundation for an individual's success in life.

Adam Patterson, Head of Early Years at the Australian International School, is equally positive, describing the Early Learning Village as a one-of-a-kind place for young children and saying that he has not worked anywhere that has paid such attention to the needs of the children who will use the space. He says that from the living walls coming to life with flowers and native bees to the shared spaces that children are finding around every corner, there is always something to discover that is exciting and that creates a sense of wonder. Parents and children do not want to go home. For Patterson, the ELV's design and intent is all about community and relationships – this is a place where lasting friendships for both children and adults are built.[2]

Superintendent Eric Sands of Stamford American International School, describes the Early Learning Village as a 'stunning' new facility, educational by design and purpose-built to give the youngest learners room to grow and space to encourage their natural curiosity.[3] Each classroom features an adjoined discovery space and is created to adapt to the changing needs

URBAN SCHOOLS: DESIGNING FOR HIGH DENSITY

Figure 4.06 Bogle Architects, ELV, Singapore, 2017 – Arrival perspective

of growing children. The outdoor learning and play zones spark imagination while the 20m swimming pool and indoor space for sports and performances enhance the physical experience for children.

COULD WE REPLICATE THIS IN THE UK?

While the sheer numbers of young children in a single school at ELV are unlikely to be replicated in this country in the near future, the challenges the ELV dealt with are the same ones many designers encounter in trying to innovate around high-density and mixed-use developments. However, what might be achievable is also dependent on the differing financial and procurement constraints of the independent and state sectors.

Regardless of budget, however, clients are often unwilling to take what they perceive to be risks; they want to see successful examples of the same ideas working elsewhere before committing to change. This is understandable, particularly where the youngest children are concerned. Cognita showed a level of trust in their educationalists and design team that allowed them to explore the challenges together and find solutions which they knew would work and could be managed. Taking the issues of circulation, safeguarding, arrival and departure, scale, pedagogy and organisation individually and creating bespoke solutions is no different to what happens on many design projects. While ELV had a level of complexity most designers do not have to consider, essentially the approach is the same. Looking to replicate a complete solution from elsewhere would not necessarily have created such a successful building, one which is completely personalised for ELV.

CONCLUSION

Many urban children are already educated in what we would consider to be tall schools of varying ages. Canon Barnett Primary School in the London Borough of Tower Hamlets, built in 1901, operates over five floors with additional mezzanine levels, and has a wonderful external rooftop learning terrace. Hampden Gurney Church of England Primary School in Westminster opened in 2002 as part of a mixed-use education and residential development, and has learning spaces over six floors with covered play areas on every level. With good design, there is no reason why young children cannot have great learning spaces in less conventional buildings. However, innovative approaches require other factors to support them, including clients who are willing to consider more radical solutions, and the right staffing levels to ensure that dispersed external learning and play areas and more complex circulation can be managed appropriately.

Many of our children already live in high-rise accommodation or large-scale developments. They look bewildered when asked for their views on high-rise schools and whether they would feel safe with, for example, open balconies or upper floor learning terraces. They ask why those spaces would be any different or less safe than the high-rise homes they live in, or the shopping centres they regularly visit. It's hard to argue with their logic.

Looking for the 'right' answer elsewhere, when it may not exist, can stifle innovation. As the Early Learning Village proves, open-minded clients and creative designers working together to develop a bespoke solution can bring forward something new and exciting that works for everyone.

CHAPTER FIVE
MIXED-USE DEVELOPMENTS

Peter Clegg & Dr Joe Jack Williams

INTRODUCTION

Under the UK Government-funded school capital initiatives Building Schools for the Future (BSF) and the previous Academies programme, there was considerable interest in schools offering a broad range of social activities, becoming more than just educational facilities. In reality schools have often done this anyway, but less deliberately and more through evolution. These adaptations could include providing a local library, sports facilities, a community hall or theatre or even a church – always responding to local needs and generally working as a shared school resource. In this way, the school adds value to the wider community.

SHARING SCHOOLS: SCHOOL AS A COMMUNITY FACILITY

Providing a facility with a clear usage for the local community, such as a sports centre, has a tangible benefit to the local area, but simply providing a space that the community can use for their specific needs can have far wider benefits than could be anticipated. Some schools use a third party to manage their buildings' out-of-hours use, such as the organisation Schools Plus, which administers the bookings and the spaces themselves. The inclusion of a third-party agent was included in Private Finance Initiative (PFI) contracts during the BSF era to secure community access. Thamesview School in Gravesend, for instance, hosts many Sikh wedding ceremonies, as the school is one of the few local buildings large enough to host the high numbers of guests expected. Without this clause in the PFI contract, this opportunity would be lost to the community, making them look further away from their neighbourhood.

In the current age of austerity, and with the chronically stretched budgets of local councils, the enhanced value of providing a school with shared facilities is especially alluring, creating an opportunity to share the cost across two projects, with potential access to separate funding pots. In the case of Academies, this could be linked to the sponsor trust, aligning the additional facilities with the school's vision or specialism, such as sports academies that require extensive pitches, halls and specialist equipment. Where schools are not able to access significant additional funding, new buildings have to be delivered at minimum cost while still providing the ability to engage with the community, presenting a significant challenge to designers.

The Plymouth School of Creative Arts (PSCA), completed in 2014, has embraced the local community's need for secure and safe spaces and hosts a very broad range of activities.

From using classrooms for external training to a regular church service on Sundays, and even hosting the regional wrestling league, the school has become a space that enables the community to be more cohesive. Where a school can become a key piece of the community, the real value of creating educational buildings can be realised: more than just social value, this can represent financial value to the school itself. Utilising the building outside of hours unlocks a substantial asset and can provide significant income; PSCA, for instance, can generate an additional £50k revenue per year from hiring out their building. While there are costs associated with hosting these events, this additional funding can be a welcome boost in an era of

Figure 5.01 FCBStudios, Plymouth School of Creative Arts – Night view

MIXED-USE DEVELOPMENTS **45**

shrinking school budgets – and increasingly necessary to balance the books.

While schools are becoming increasingly aware of the potential for out-of-hours use of their buildings, it is important to understand how the building can be zoned to enable this.

Defining other uses in the brief is the best way of ensuring they are compatible, and this has to be strategically incorporated at an early stage. Perhaps the most obvious example is the inclusion of secure routes between entrances and facilities, enabling the rest of the school

Figure 5.02 FCB Studios, St Mary's RC Primary School, Battersea- Zoning Plan.

yellow = school
blue = housing
→ = access routes
┅ = parent waiting zones

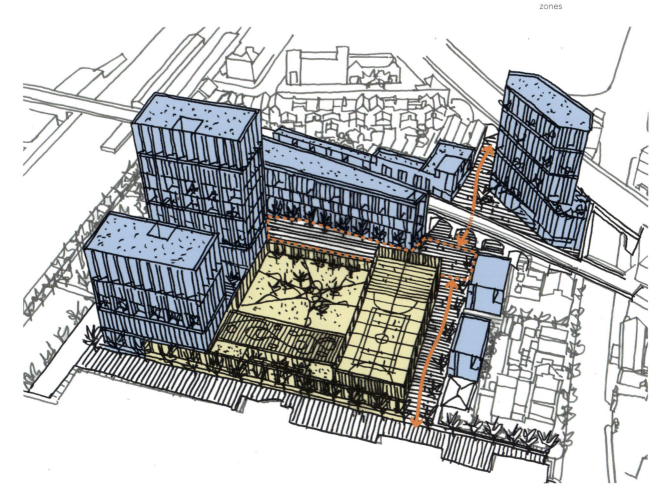

to be locked down while the event runs. Also important are the support spaces, such as toilets, needed to serve the main bookable space. The community spaces must be able to function as a complete and separate entity to ensure full utilisation.

FUNDING SCHOOLS: SCHOOLS AS PART OF WIDER DEVELOPMENTS

In cities across England, new housing developments currently being constructed tend to have high densities to ensure that they remain financially viable. While these developments are essential to provide much-needed homes, they can put undue stress on local facilities, including schools. Many local authorities have school systems that are over-subscribed even prior to the influx of new homes, and need to provide space for the additional students. Through planning obligations, councils are able to levy funding on new developments to help relieve the school place shortage in the form of a Community Infrastructure Levy (CIL) or a Section 106 (S106) agreement. Both effectively require a payment, either in cash or in kind, that can then be used to improve local facilities, in this case being put towards school places. CIL funding can be used throughout the local borough on any infrastructure project that the council requires, including schools. S106 agreements require that the funding be used to enable the development to provide an amenity, typically on or around the site, that the council declares is essential to the success of development within the local community. Unlike CIL, S106 payments tend to be negotiated with the council, ensuring the development remains financially viable.

By contrast, CIL levy rates are usually set as a standard charge across the borough or council.

Commonly, the greatest opportunity that arises from either CIL or S106 is that the development site itself can be used to provide a school; otherwise, the cost of land within these areas would often be prohibitively expensive for the council and the national Education and Skills Funding Agency (ESFA) to provide a school. In London, land prices are on average £7,700 per square metre,[1] nearly six times the construction cost funding available for a school through the ESFA (in FCBStudios' experience, this tends to be around £1,350 per m^2); in boroughs such as Kensington & Chelsea, land costs can rise to over 14 times the standard construction costs. Funding for land typically sits outside ESFA funding, and this cost presents the principal difficulty a council faces when trying to establish a new school within its borough. Any land that is owned by the council is likely to be in high demand, due to the pressure to create more homes and the prospect of alleviating the stretched budgets through land sale. For many councils, it is the access to land that would otherwise be unattainable that is the greatest opportunity of a new development. Using the negotiation around S106, in particular, enables the creation of a mixed-use development, providing the school on the available site and satisfying the need for increased school places and more homes. This is subject to affordability analysis by the developer, but the increasing number of mixed-use developments, particularly in London, show that this is a viable route.

Negotiating a school to be part of the development can be beneficial not just for the council but also for the developer: councils will be providing those school spaces that they could not otherwise afford, and the developer is building a school within walking distance of their housing. The addition of a good school has been shown to increase prices for homes in the catchment area, potentially increasing returns for the developer and further reducing their risk. Schools can become the focal point for a new development, creating a centre that may not otherwise naturally arise and around which a community can form. This is apparent not just with housing developments, but also with retail projects, most notably at the Deer Park School in Richmond. This new primary school is part of a development led by supermarket Lidl, with the school occupying the first and second floors of the building, above Lidl's retail premises. The family-orientated nature of Richmond has meant that the local schools are full or overfull, so through working with an expanding retailer the local community not only receives a new shop, but also a much-needed school that would be otherwise difficult to fund.

The high value of land also means that many schools in desirable areas have now found

Figure 5.03 Kier Construction: Deer Park School, Richmond – Visualisation

themselves sitting on a valuable asset. The land value of many schools, including their playing fields, is an enticing opportunity for many to fund a new building and transform their learning environment. When plots neighbouring the Holy Trinity School in Dalston were developed into high-density luxury flats, the school spotted an opportunity to improve their low-rise, poor-quality building. Rock Townsend Architects designed a new school to be incorporated into the lower two floors of a residential apartment building. With a rooftop play area on the second floor of the building, the housing itself provides cover to this important external space.

The value in the land of existing schools has been recognised by the UK Government, which has set up a new organisation, LocatED, to act as an in-house developer helping schools unlock additional funding. However, selling off school land is not a decision taken lightly, and needs approval from the Secretary of State for Education. Providing outdoor spaces for the students is incredibly important, particularly in areas where there are limited opportunities for outdoor play, and a short-sighted focus on money can have repercussions that will last far longer than any funding raised.

Figure 5.04 Rock Townsend Architects, Holy Trinity Primary School, Dalston, 2016

MIXED-USE DEVELOPMENTS

Figure 5.05 Rock Townsend Architects, Holy Trinity Primary School, Dalston, 2016

SCHOOLS AND HOMES: BALANCING NEEDS

Within mixed-use developments, the ideal solution is often to physically separate the school and housing. This enables the school to be delivered apart from the housing, allowing each to have flexibility in procurement and construction methods and reducing the risk to the overall development. It also reduces potential future complexities, notably around maintenance and servicing, and simplifying future adaptation to buildings. This physical separation also provides a greater delineation between the housing and school, increasing their identities. However, this division is not always possible; high-density sites in particular may necessitate an overlap of building footprints, either partially (such as at St Mary's

RC Primary School in Battersea) or entirely, as at Deer Park School or the Holy Trinity School. The viability of the mixed-use scheme resides in producing a design that will enable all the uses to coexist harmoniously.

Embedding schools within high-density developments brings with it a set of potential conflicts that need careful management to ensure successful schemes. The first aspect to consider is how to locate the school within the development: will the students be coming from the new homes, from the surrounding areas, or both? The type of housing and expected occupants will have an impact on the school location: a development with many smaller units will likely be filled with young professionals and unlikely to have children that attend local schools, whereas developments containing larger, multi-bed units, particularly where there is a social housing provision, can be expected to contribute students to the on-site school. Such information, as well as general demographic projections, is key when sizing a new school, working with the local authority plan and understanding whether the new school building is for an entirely new school, expanding a local school, or simply providing modern facilities for an existing school.

Where the school is likely to serve existing communities, and particularly where it is replacing an existing school, then it can become a beacon to draw people into the development, increasing social cohesion between the new and existing. Routes to the school should be considered from the outset, since a school creates regular and sizeable traffic volumes at either end of the day. The level of traffic relates to the source of the students mentioned earlier – there will be different impacts depending on whether they are from the surrounding development, nearby, or from further afield. Typically, most schools prefer one entrance that can be easily managed for security and safeguarding, which naturally creates a focus for the routes through the development; these can be especially noisy paths and should avoid directly passing too close to homes. Widening the key routes means noise during arrival and departure is less concentrated and more easily dissipated, reducing disruption to any surrounding homes.

Within multi-use developments, it is often desirable to remove traffic from within the development and force it to the perimeter. This provides a safer environment for the community and will also improve local air quality. Schools in areas of high pollution are already looking at restrictions on dropping students off using cars, moving the drop-off point further from the school itself. For future developments, schools should encourage students to use less polluting, more sustainable methods of transport, such as walking or cycling.

The space around the entrance should be relatively open, supporting the safeguarding of the students by the school, but it is a key transition space for the students and parents, particularly at primary schools. This is often the point where parents and teachers can interact informally, building relationships to support the students. Where schools encourage meeting, fixed seating can provide space to linger and can relax the interaction, making social contact between parents easier. At St Mary's RC School in Battersea, for instance, the main entrance (containing communal seating) is in the centre of the new development, encouraging parents and children to move through the housing. At the end of the school day, the communal seating is taken up with parents waiting to pick up their children, filling the square with life and vibrancy at a time that would otherwise be quiet. However, its placement on the edge of the boundary still provides the school with a street presence, permitting it to have its own distinct identity.

This area for interaction outside the school is not always welcomed. Some schools and local authorities prefer to avoid a risk of confrontation between teachers and parents, particularly when issues of student discipline arise. This decision can underpin the philosophy of the site, governing the location of the school entrance and routes for student movement through the development. Moving the entrance to the perimeter of the site will significantly reduce the noise of students travelling to and from

MIXED-USE DEVELOPMENTS | 51

Figure 5.06 FCBStudios, St Mary's RC Primary School, Battersea, 2016

the school within the development, as well as increasing the visibility of the school to the wider community.

As with the access routes, a school's outside areas need to be carefully considered, particularly when the cost of any additional land used is factored in. There are several external areas suggested by the ESFA Building Bulletin 103 guidance; however, it is obvious that providing playing fields in

URBAN SCHOOLS: DESIGNING FOR HIGH DENSITY

Figure 5.07 FCBStudios, St Mary's RC Primary School, Battersea, 2016

cities is unlikely, a fact acknowledged by the space standards. Instead, the focus is on hard informal social areas and hard PE space, with other spaces more readily available outside the development (usually local sports centres or playing fields). A typical solution is to locate the hard PE space (a multi-use games area, or MUGA) on top of the school, with the necessary rectilinear shape matching the layout of the internal school sports hall. The less structured social spaces can then be accommodated around the rest of the building, using small courtyards and roof space to create a varied area for use during breaks and lunch. These spaces need to be designed with an openness that enables simple supervision, either passively from inside the school or by a small number of staff. Using the roof of the school increases the value of that land under the school, not only providing teaching, but also social space. At Chelsea Academy, for instance, the land available for the school was so restricted that the buildings filled the whole of the site and most of the roof spaces were designed to provide a variety of outdoor play spaces. Typically this would preclude the school and the housing sharing a footprint, but at the new Holy Trinity School development, the housing begins above the provided 'rooftop' play space.

Schools are inherently noisy places, and during breaks the noise escalates. But this is an important part of the school day: the extra energy students burn helps them settle during lessons, as well as allowing them to develop their social skills. Placing the school on the edge of the development and using the school itself to shield the homes from most of the noise is a successful mitigation route; noise is channelled away from the homes provided by the development itself. Using a courtyard for outdoor social space provides more opportunities for noise reduction than using the roof spaces, which would require the building of high parapet walls to achieve the same attenuation to neighbouring spaces.

Understanding and managing the overlooking of a school is a priority for the design within a high-density development. There is considerable, justified nervousness at providing homes that look directly into schools. While the risk to vulnerable children these homes create is real, however, the true scale of that risk is hard to quantify. Many schools have operated in urban areas with considerable 'overlooking' for many years, and some see it as building a positive relationship, but to understand the risk it is important to liaise with local Secured by Design officers who can establish the site's particular needs. A useful starting point is to think in terms of privacy and reasonableness. There may be homes that overlook the school, but their sightlines can be limited, potentially by elevating them much higher than the school and using trees with large canopies to break up any views. Similarly, windows from a school should not look directly into the windows of homes, but should instead be angled to reduce the natural view. Staggering levels between the school and other buildings is effective at preventing casual views between the spaces, ensuring that homes feel sufficiently private but also that the children remain safeguarded. As with many elements of school design, the level of transparency between the school and its surroundings is governed by how the school wants to sit within the community, and this needs to be established early in the design process.

High-density developments can have a tendency to become a series of tall buildings, leading to severe overshadowing around the base of the tower. Maintaining a compact form for the schools means many end up at only a few storeys high, and could be in the shadow of the much taller blocks of homes they are there to support. Careful solar analysis of the impact of nearby homes and the school is necessary to ensure that the school remains full of daylight and, more importantly, keeps the students in the school connected to the outside. The location of the school on the site clearly needs to take the neighbouring sites into account, but in general, in the UK, placing the school towards the south and east of the site will enable it to gain the most in terms of sunlight during the open hours for the school, without overshadowing housing. While it is tempting to place the school at the heart of the development, limitations on overshadowing can reduce the height of towers to the south of the school, drastically reducing the number of units and hence the financial viability of the scheme.

With any mixed-use development there is a tension between the various elements of the design and establishing which takes priority over the others. On a site containing both housing and schools, each is clearly dependent on the other – but it is often unclear which should take priority. Priorities will vary from site to site, taking into account the school's brief and the main client/developer's aspirations. Ideally, both housing and schools would be equally important on the site; in practice, the overwhelming value of housing can skew priorities away from schools, which can lead to schools being overshadowed, squeezed or sidelined, and outdoor spaces or aspect (or both) being severely compromised. Careful design of the relationship of home to school can add value to both and create successful mixed-use developments characteristic of what we think of as healthy and liveable cities.

CONCLUSION

Mixed-use development is becoming increasingly prevalent, as land prices in cities continue to increase and council budgets shrink. There are some very good reasons to build mixed-use developments, but there are also some key pitfalls to avoid.

Figure 5.08 David Morley Architects, Kings Cross Academy and Frank Barnes School for Deaf Children, London, 2015 – Cross-section of the apartments over the school

PROS AND CONS OF MIXED-USE DEVELOPMENTS

Pros

1. Schools give new residential communities a social focus.
2. The convenience of a school within walking distance reduces reliance on motorised transport.
3. Good schools can add value to nearby family homes.
4. Significant cost savings can be realised with shared overheads between the two developments.
5. Higher-density development results in increased site utilisation with higher value achieved.
6. Funding from the residential elements can drive higher-quality buildings.
7. Shared services between homes and school can allow large-scale, energy efficient servicing systems.

Cons

1. Schools can get 'buried' in larger developments and lack their own identity or presence.
2. Overlooking and safeguarding issues can cause problems if not designed out.
3. Rights to light and overshadowing from high-density developments can create poor daylighting.
4. Lack of outdoor space that belongs to the school should not be an acceptable compromise, particularly for an urban school.
5. Procurement route for school and housing can be complex.

CHAPTER SIX
HIGH-RISE SCHOOLS

Helen Taylor

INTRODUCTION

New skyscrapers are being added to global city skylines each year. With the need for further schools in cities, it is only a matter of time before educational learning within tall buildings becomes more commonplace. The solution to providing schools in densely populated areas of the city has long been to build high: the hundreds of London Board Schools built at the end of the 19th century, many of which still operate, are examples. Seen through the fictional gaze of Sherlock Holmes, these were signals of a bright and better future:

> 'Look at those big, isolated clumps of building rising up above the slates, like brick islands in a lead-colored sea.'
> 'The board-schools.'
> Light-houses, my boy! Beacons of the future! Capsules with hundreds of bright little seeds in each, out of which will spring the wise, better England of the future…'[1]

TALL BUILDINGS

Verticality is ingrained in our ways of thinking about education. It has been established since the state elected to take responsibility for the compulsory education of its citizens. School buildings in urban areas were built high, with the youngest children occupying the ground floor and moving up as they aged. In a 1937 documentary directed by John Grierson, *Children at School*, a graphic is used to explain to the imagined parent-viewer how, starting from nursery, the infant progresses ever upwards to the rooftop of an imagined building from where they will go on to either work or university. In the 21st century, verticality continues to signal commitment and investment. The visibility of these structures rising above the surrounding rooftops reassures the onlooker that education is secure and is happening.

What do we mean by high-rise schools? Four or five storeys is no longer unusual, so we are referring here to six storeys and

URBAN SCHOOLS: DESIGNING FOR HIGH DENSITY

above. A height of 18m, roughly six storeys, is historically linked with the reach capability of fire and rescue service equipment such as wheeled escape ladders. What we think of as high-rise in a school is dwarfed by the tall, super-tall and mega-tall structures emerging around the world. The tallest building currently recognised is the Burj Khalifa in UAE with 163 storeys, while the tallest education building is the Mode Gakuen Cocoon Tower, a university building in Tokyo, each of whose 50 floors contains rectangular classrooms with a student lounge on every third floor.[2] With residential apartments now located 85 storeys above ground in New York, maybe in the future all buildings above 30 storeys high should integrate educational provision?

Precedents of tall schools around the world are limited. The majority of city centre multi-storey schools are operated privately, with funding and organisation varying between each. Examples include the ten-storey Avenues: The World School in New York, which was converted from a 1928 Cass Gilbert designed warehouse, and the seven-storey Botanic High School in Adelaide which opened recently and caters for 1,250 secondary school students.

CASE STUDIES

Three multi-storey schools offer case studies. One, the unbuilt ten-storey SHaW Futures Academy in Bromley, South-East London, prompted the development of this book: although the development has halted due to local planning issues, the project offers a useful example of how to resolve curriculum delivery and pupil management in a multi-storey school environment. The eight-storey William Jones College Preparatory High School in Chicago, recently rebuilt on a long-established tight city-centre site, provides a useful precedent in terms of height, organisation and pedagogical strategies, while the six-storey Bobby Moore Academy, opened in September 2018 in Stratford, East London, demonstrates how curriculum and behavioural expectations in the UK have been successfully accommodated in a stacked arrangement.

Figures 6.01 and 6.02
Bonetti/Kozerski in collaboration with Perkins Eastman Architects, Avenues, The World School, New York City, 2012

HIGH-RISE SCHOOLS | 59

URBAN SCHOOLS: DESIGNING FOR HIGH DENSITY

CASE STUDY: SHaW Futures Academy, London

Imagined as a landmark as part of the wider regeneration of the Bromley area, SHaW Futures was designed to be a centre for Science, Health and Wellbeing excellence, offering 11- to 19-year-olds unrivalled access to skills and opportunities on their front doorstep. The design drivers and vision were aspirational:

- A tool for learning and excitement in daily school life
- Laboratory and specialist spaces on show and dispersed
- Flexibility to adapt the curriculum linked with industry
- Shared spaces at the heart
- An 'active front' to interact and integrate with the surroundings and encourage community use
- Creation of 'learning neighbourhoods'
- Inclusive design throughout in terms of access, facilities and safe emergency evacuation

'*The unusual site gave us the opportunity to innovate with a non-traditional learning environment that was more reflective of a work place or office environment and fit with the vocational and work related aspirations of our students. After working through the designs with our architects we became more convinced that the practical flow, space and utilisation constraints and concerns were easily overcome with innovative design features that have created an education space more akin to an adult working environment and this really fits with the ethos of the school.*
Sam Parrett OBE, Group Principal & CEO, London and South East Education Group

Design innovation was needed to meet UK Government school standards while potential solutions were constrained by site conditions, many of which were invisible: an unbridgeable culvert under the site; local height, massing and building line restrictions; protected views; and the site's position at the junction between high-rise commercial and low-rise suburban residential development. With no similar UK precedents in operation to assess during the design process in 2016, the client team carried out detailed timetabling exercises to ensure efficiency and flexibility in the circulation and accommodation and allow for any unanticipated future needs of the school.

The site constraints necessitated a multi-storey solution. A pragmatic design response was needed on the lower floors where plans

Figure 6.03 Scott Brownrigg, SHaW Futures Academy, Bromley – Front entrance visualisation

CASE STUDY: SHaW Futures Academy, London (CONTINUED)

show a relatively deep-plan 'podium' (four storeys from lower and upper ground to Level 2) accommodating larger-volume spaces such as the main hall and activity studio, or fully enclosed spaces such as changing rooms and stores. Teaching spaces are kept to the perimeter for daylight and views, while internal rooms are limited to circulation, some staff bases and small group rooms where staff and students spend less lengthy periods. In the more 'rational' upper block (six storeys from Levels 3 to 8), the narrower floorplate was designed to permit direct access to daylight throughout. A central void in the slab for an accommodation stair brings borrowed light deep into the heart of the plan. Corridors are avoided, and all circulation and social spaces benefit from natural daylight and views.

Building in flexibility was challenging due to the vertical stacking of accommodation and the need to retain appropriate fire escape provision. However, the proposed use of a concrete frame structure with flat slabs and minimal load-bearing partitions allowed for potential internal re-planning. A variety of room sizes and shapes was provided on every floor to encourage alternative classroom layouts and a

Figure 6.04 Scott Brownrigg, SHaW Futures Academy, Bromley – High street view visualisation

CASE STUDY: SHaW Futures Academy, London (CONTINUED)

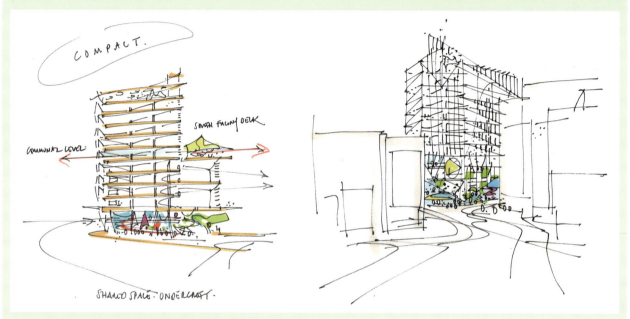

Figure 6.05 Scott Brownrigg, SHaW Futures Academy, Bromley – Concept sketches

natural diversity of teaching spaces. Specialist spaces require flexible use to meet timetabling requirements, which in turn generates a more standardised Furniture, Fittings and Equipment (FFE) installation that can be used in different ways. This flexibility allowed for the curriculum to develop, and for the timetabling of facilities to start on the lower floors and expand up the building as the school population grew over time.

A tall school requires a significantly greater proportion and area of circulation than a typical three- or four-storey school, so the provision of adequate teaching space without exceeding the total funded area was a critical challenge. To minimise excessive travel distances during the school day the vertical layout effectively creates three stacked schools (one for each Key Stage), each with its own dining and social space, learning resource centre, and external space.

Key Stage 3 students (Years 7 and 8 – ages 11 to 13) arrive at the Lower Ground Floor, under the 'bridge' into the external play area, where their dining area creates a social space. They take the stairs to their Learning Bases on the Upper Ground Floor, Level 1 and Level 2 where a series of general classrooms, Science Labs, Music, Activity Studio, Food and Resistant Material spaces allow for the delivery of a broad and balanced curriculum. A Sports Science Lab and Computing Base ensure the younger students can also experience the high-quality specialist spaces on offer in the school and see older students learning on a daily basis.

Key Stage 4 students (Years 9, 10 and 11 – ages 13 to 16) arrive by the main entrance at the Upper Ground Floor and take the central stairs or lifts to their Hub at Level 3. Levels 4, 5, 6 and 7 contain a range of specialist and general teaching spaces to deliver the three learning pathways on offer. These pupils share some of these spaces with students aged over 16, allowing collaboration across the phases and for older students to act as role models. Flexible areas for skills development and independent study, as well as the highly specialist spaces for Health, Biomedical and Sports, Computing and Electronics, allow

HIGH-RISE SCHOOLS

CASE STUDY: SHaW Futures Academy, London (CONTINUED)

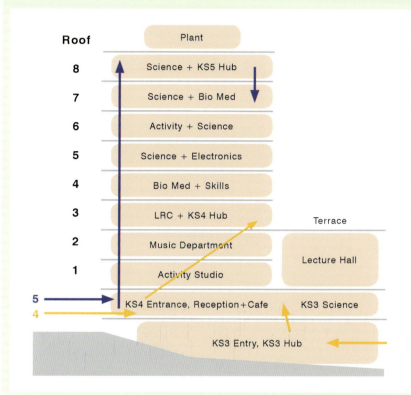

Figure 6.06 Scott Brownrigg, SHaW Futures Academy, Bromley – Stacked Key Stage hubs

for practice-based education for all learners to develop problem-solving abilities and communication skills.

Key Stage 5 students (Years 12 and 13 – ages 16 to 19) also arrive via the Upper Ground Floor entrance and take the north core lifts to their social space at Level 8. In the Sixth Form, highly specialist pathways will be established with employers focused on Science, Health and Wellbeing.

These Key Stage Learning Bases create a sense of identity, community and progression as students move through the school. They also allow for each curriculum area to have a core cluster of learning spaces within the building, enabling them to form a clear identity, showcase career opportunities, display student work and allow staff to share practice.

Circulation was designed to provide comfortable vertical and horizontal flow, but also opportunities for informal group work and connectivity. In order that students felt safe and secure at all times, staff spaces were placed for maximum passive supervision and pupil- and staff-accessible toilets were evenly distributed on every floor for ease of access.

Key spaces such as the main entrances from the high street and through the bridge, the café at the entrance, the main hall and science labs would be on show, ensuring the school would be visibly at the heart of the neighbourhood – a beacon of learning.

However, although the proposal was recommended for approval and supported by the client and the Commission for Architecture and the Built Environment (CABE), the proposal was turned down at planning appeal. While the site was allocated for a tall building and educational use in the local plan, there was neighbourhood concern about pupil management, safety and means of escape, in a climate of concern particularly heightened by the recent Grenfell Tower fire. Delivering a locally acceptable building form that managed the necessary transition from a ten-storey structure to the neighbouring two-storey residential buildings required more flexibility in the procurement process and design parameters than the team had available. The site continues to be owned and used for education by the Department for Education.

A hint at the perception of the project was contained in an article in the local newspaper, which noted of the proposed school: 'It would have been slightly shorter than the great pyramid at Giza and the Washington Monument.'[3]

CASE STUDY: William Jones College Preparatory High School, Chicago

William Jones College Preparatory High School is Chicago's best-performing public school. Its new eight-storey building came about as the existing six-storey 1960s building had become outdated and no longer provided appropriate accessible facilities for the school, particularly for its successful performing arts programme, and was too small to meet the demand for pupil places. The new school was designed for 1,200 students, but in the end it was merged with the old, enabling pupil numbers to expand from the original 800 to a current capacity of 1,800.

The school site in downtown Chicago is surrounded by high-rise buildings There was no restriction on its potential height placed by its context; however, the City of Chicago has a 'prototype' school design – based on three-storey accommodation on a playing field – which model had to be adapted and stacked on this site. The 'jelly diagrams' in Figure 6.08 illustrate how the accommodation has been arranged, with the theatre at ground level due to legal requirements and the shared sports spaces located with amazing views at the top of the building. The apparent simplicity of the adjacencies disguises some major technical challenges, but getting this arrangement right for the school has been key to its success. Locating classrooms in the middle storeys, with shared resources above and below, minimises day-to-day circulation and creates a span that ties everything together. With no room for green space at street level, the school provides access to outside terraces at numerous levels above ground, and makes the most of the benefits of the city, creating visual and physical connections to a great park and playing fields nearby. The school also benefits from world-class cultural institutions on the nearby museum campus – the Art Institute of Chicago, Field Museum and Adler Planetarium – meaning it can use the city as a fantastic learning opportunity. In return, the school gives back to the city by offering after-hours civic amenities.

The design of the school makes the most of its location at the termination of a street that provides a critical route into Grant Park and the world-renowned Lake Shore Drive. The school entrance and 'Commons' have been located at this prime node, blending into the context and view of major hotels nearby. This creates a civic presence with extensive transparency that supports both a sense of safety and the relationship to the city. The Commons itself is an atrium space at the heart of the school that relates to both the street and the centre of the building. Such spaces – which celebrate arrival and circulation and aid wayfinding – are important and should not be considered an optional extra; they provide a vital threshold between the city and school, helping students to adjust at the start and end of a day, and reinforcing a sense of place and community.

The Chicago Public Building Commission led the process and, despite the unusual

Figure 6.07 Perkins + Will Architects, William Jones College Prep, Chicago, 2013 – The site of adjacent new and retained school buildings

HIGH-RISE SCHOOLS   65

CASE STUDY: William Jones College Preparatory High School, Chicago (*CONTINUED*)

Figure 6.08 Perkins + Will Architects, William Jones College, Chicago, 2013 – 'Jelly diagrams' illustrating adjacencies

nature of the design, parity with other public schools was important. Despite their minimal involvement at that stage, the teaching staff are reportedly very happy with the outcome. The architect suspects this may have been helped by Jones College being a progressive school, and its teachers long accustomed to working in an urban multi-storey environment. There was concern about the need for students to walk up seven floors, and travel distances have been increased by the retention of the existing school as additional accommodation; this has been accommodated by an adjusted teaching schedule. The architect, meanwhile, reports that the school is proud to have the fittest students in the district.

Figure 6.09 Perkins + Will Architects, William Jones College Prep, Chicago, 2013 – The 'Commons' at the entrance

Figure 6.10 Perkins + Will Architects, William Jones College Prep, Chicago, 2013 – Central staircase

URBAN SCHOOLS: DESIGNING FOR HIGH DENSITY

CASE STUDY: Bobby Moore Academy, London

Opened in 2018 in the heart of the Queen Elizabeth Olympic Park in East London, Bobby Moore Academy provides 'all-through' education comprising separate primary and secondary school buildings and sports facilities. Specialisms in science and sport capitalise on the world-class sports facilities provided by the legacy of the 2012 Olympics. Community access is offered for dining, gathering, assembly hall, music and IT teaching, alongside the sports hall, fitness suite, dance studio and changing rooms on the lower floors, with an extra-large lift to accommodate parasports teams. At the upper levels, the school is organised by faculty, floor by floor, with science at the top.

The 3,500m² site is triangular in shape, bounded by roads and the adjacent Olympic Stadium's running track and practice pitch, so a multi-storey solution was the only option. A number of key features address this constraint:

- The building is positioned along the northern boundary, maximising south-facing play space.
- A shared surface in front of the school creates a pedestrian-friendly public realm and a safe gathering space at the beginning and end of the school day.
- The large main spaces – the assembly hall and sports hall – are raised to the first floor, providing outdoor covered social space at ground level and allowing large areas of glazing to maximise transparency and views through the school.
- A series of roof terraces step up the rear elevation to provide additional external south-facing social space, commanding distant views over Central London and Canary Wharf.

Despite its small site and compact form, it is a building of generous proportions, organised around a wide internal 'street' punctuated by voids to connect each level and provide daylight deep into the plan from skylights above. A central triple-height atrium forms the heart and focus of the school and provides

Figure 6.11 Penoyre & Prasad, Bobby Moore Academy, London, 2018 – On the banks of the City Mill River, commanding views over the Olympic Park to the north and central London to the south

HIGH-RISE SCHOOLS   67

CASE STUDY: Bobby Moore Academy, London (CONTINUED)

Section A - A
1. Dining Hall
2. Auditorium
3. Terrace
4. English Dept.
5. Humanities Dept.
6. Science Dept.

Section B - B
1. Drama Studio
2. Main Hall
3. Dining Hall
4. Library
5. Sports Hall
6. Activity Studio
7. Terrace

Figure 6.12 Penoyre & Prasad, Bobby Moore Academy, London, 2018 – Section drawing

orientation along the internal street's length. Above this sits a double-height library, with a roof terrace above. A triple-height sports hall and double-height assembly hall and drama studio are inserted as distinctive volumes at first floor, while a double-height dance studio 'bookends' the building at one end. Windows and screens maximise transparency and views through and into these spaces.

The school's strong architectural expression presents a bold civic presence to the Park and complements the surrounding iconic Olympic legacy buildings. Maximising the amount of on-site play space and securing exclusive access and visual links to adjacent and nearby

CASE STUDY: Bobby Moore Academy, London (CONTINUED)

specialist sports facilities allayed parents' concerns about the lack of outdoor play space, which is now boosted by timetabled outdoor learning.

Generous circulation and bold design have been critical to the success of the school. The 4m wide corridors allow pupils to pass each other easily and to wait outside their classrooms before lessons. The bright, wide staircases mitigate against congestion and feature bold colours and numbers to support orientation and identity. Extensive use of glazed screens allows views from and through the classrooms, brings daylight into the corridors and ensures passive supervision at all times. The shared architectural identity with the primary school helps students transitioning from the primary to the secondary school to feel more at home and the students are particularly keen on the bright yellow colour palette, which is carried across both school sites.

Figure 6.13 Penoyre & Prasad, Bobby Moore Academy, London, 2018 – The atrium forms the heart of the school

Figure 6.14 Penoyre & Prasad, Bobby Moore Academy, London, 2018 – A new public realm has been created in front of the school.

CONCLUSION

What was clear from the outset of the development of SHaW's innovative design, and is evident in the other case studies, was the importance of the commitment of the school trust to a multi-storey environment. Architecturally, these schools also share the same clear priorities for success:

- Generous, attractive and safe horizontal and vertical circulation and arrival space
- Transparency and good passive supervision
- A building frontage on the street with a pedestrian-friendly public realm, and gathering spaces to encourage social interaction
- Optimised opportunities for outside space within the site and building, both on and above ground, and visual links to the city around them
- Secure and guaranteed access arrangements for schools' use of shared community and sports facilities
- A strong architectural identity making a positive contribution to its urban context

Any school regardless of shape and size would benefit from these principles.

These new multi-storey schools may have been designed to respond to physical and economic constraints, but they also offer a fantastic opportunity to integrate education into the heart of a city and to implement and progress new ways of learning. While the principle of creating sustainable cities with a social infrastructure that accommodates children and families is becoming an accepted requirement worldwide, there is still resistance to educating children in multi-storey environments.

High-rise schools need to be developed in the context of an integrated policy approach to a child-friendly urban infrastructure that ensures access to suitable housing, parks and the natural world. Funding and procurement that accommodate a non-standard approach and elements like wide stairs and roof terraces must be considered from the outset, while a more holistic approach could address common local community concerns. If urbanisation continues as predicted, tall schools are unlikely to remain rare.

A city-centre multi-storey school should not be a poor choice for children. William Jones College in Chicago consistently ranks among the top high schools in the city, state and country, based on multiple measures of student success. With a history stretching back 150 years, the school and its facilities have evolved over time to meet changing educational needs. The school is both for the city and of the city.

CHAPTER SEVEN

REUSE, REPURPOSE, SHARE

Michael Buchanan

INTRODUCTION

The lack of available sites for new schools to meet unprecedented demand for places has resulted in the emergence of a national (indeed international) debate and narrative around reimagining urban schools and how a school is defined. New thinking challenges orthodoxies about how spaces are configured: no longer is a school necessarily seen as a freestanding, purpose-built establishment.

This paucity of suitable sites has prompted an examination of whether existing redundant or underused buildings might be adaptively reused and repurposed. There are numerous examples of imaginative design solutions that transform repurposed buildings into inspirational learning spaces, although significant problems have also been encountered. In this chapter we look specifically at some of the opportunities and challenges of providing education environments in buildings not originally designed as schools.

SUITABILITY AND COST CONSIDERATIONS

Not every building can be turned into an effective school, regardless of the available budget. Choice of building and objective analysis of its suitability are key. A suitability assessment needs to consider technical feasibility, economic viability and functionality as a learning environment. Some technical considerations were identified by Atkins in its publication *Refresh, Refurbish, Remodel, Reuse*:

> *Changing the use of an existing building and turning it into a suitable learning environment is no mean feat. The main challenges to be faced include the layout of existing buildings; the capacity and efficiency of existing services and systems; ability to comply with current legislative requirements; the energy efficiency of the building fabric; overall site layout and constraints.*[1]

Michael E. Hall of AIA, quoted in the US publication *Building Design and Construction*, points out that 'nearly all conversion projects require complete replacement of the existing mechanical systems to meet the air quality and changeover requirements of school environments. Therefore, high ceilings are a must. Big boxes and warehouse buildings typically provide more than enough clearance height for classrooms, but historical structures and strip malls may not.'[2]

One of the technical challenges often encountered is creating sufficient natural daylighting. The former use of many redundant buildings, for example offices or commercial premises, rarely required the level of daylighting required for learning activities; space-efficiency and cost drivers resulted in 'deep plan' designs. Retrospectively ensuring sufficient daylight penetration in such buildings requires extensive remodelling, if not structural alterations – for example, enlarging fenestration openings, cutting through floors to create light wells or providing glazed panels for borrowed light. All these alterations increase cost, potentially significantly.

Retaining and reconfiguring an existing building should be more sustainable, but the assumption that this would be more cost-effective should be questioned. Firstly, a significant cost risk lies in what the contractor finds only when intrusive work begins: some of

Figure 7.01 Working with the fabric of an existing building

REUSE, REPURPOSE, SHARE

the structure and fabric may prove to be beyond their operational life, or contaminants such as asbestos may be encountered. Secondly, repurposing an existing building inevitably requires upgrading of facilities and infrastructure to meet current building performance standards for factors such as daylighting, thermal comfort, air quality, acoustics and energy efficiency. In a new building, these factors are designed in, using modern products, with close consideration of installation, routings of services and so on, often using technology such as Building Information Modelling (BIM).

In existing buildings, these systems need to be retrofitted; even where this is possible, it can be disproportionately expensive and still result in less than fully effective performance.

Eden Girls' School in Slough, an Islamic faith secondary free school for the Star Academy Trust (formerly Tauheedul Education Trust) had a thorough makeover at seemingly reasonable cost. With façade and glazing retained, the building was stripped back to its steel frame and a feature staircase inserted to improve circulation and light penetration. However, when the cost of acquiring the building was

Figure 7.02 ADP Architects, Eden Girls' School, Slough – The inserted toplit staircase

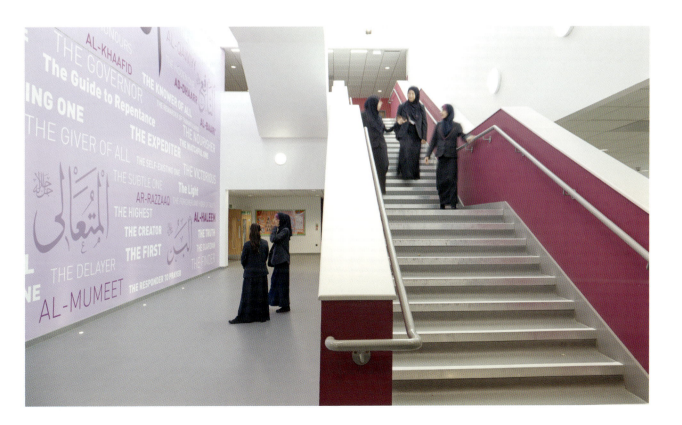

included, the total cost was roughly equivalent to that of building new on a clear site. Financial assessment of an existing building's lifecycle, renewal and maintenance obligations and energy use needs to be made alongside the capital cost of conversion.

FUNCTIONALITY CONSIDERATIONS

In terms of suitability as a learning environment, repurposing existing buildings presents both challenges and opportunities, and decisions need to be made around organisational and pedagogical intents. Innovative curricula, school organisation and modes of learning can be found in many free schools in the UK and charter schools in the US, made possible as both are state-maintained but not directly accountable to local authorities or school boards. When such schools encourage flexible, collaborative learning, for example, the need for more open, flexible spaces and different sizes of space present design possibilities for some building typologies that a more traditional organisational model would not. Hence the functionality assessment needs to be based on a mature, resolved and well-understood educational brief.

Dr Kaisa Nuikkinen, Head Architect for School Design at Helsinki City Education Department, Finland, sees the school building itself as an intrinsic part of the learning experience, arguing that not only is economic viability important but the highest quality of architecture is needed because you 'can't separate learning from physical environments'. She poses the question: 'Does the school act as a three-dimensional textbook?', suggesting it should provide starting points for the curriculum and 'nooks and crannies to reflect on what we have learnt'.[3]

The acquisition by the Education and Skills Funding Agency (the delivery agency for the Department for Education in England) of a number of surplus police stations in London for conversion into schools seems to be an opportunity to secure urban sites for much-needed schools. However, the building typology is very specific and constraining, and some examples illustrate a mismatch between educational requirements and the building form. The structure, design and specification of the former South Norwood police station reconfigured for Harris Aspire Academy, for example, is a deep-plan building, with little daylight ingress and oppressively low ceiling heights. Architects ADP had to overcome the difficulties of a (literally) bombproof structure, the cost of demolition on a tight urban site which would only allow one vehicle movement at a time, 100% mechanical ventilation and a lot of the accommodation being in the former basement car park, with no views out and a reliance on artificial daylight.

Typically very few of these converted buildings provide the space for play and sports required by Sport England. To achieve permission to operate, schools usually make service-level agreements with external organisations – playing fields, sports centres and other schools and colleges – to provide for physical education and sport off-site. This has long-term consequences for timetabling, cost and transport.

PEDAGOGY-LED DESIGN: OPPORTUNITIES FOR INDUSTRIAL BUILDINGS

A common feature of many schools operating successfully in converted buildings is that they are free schools, charter schools, university technical colleges, studio schools and the like, and tend to be small scale, standing outside the traditional mainstream – innovating both the curriculum and their pedagogical and organisational models. These schools can be more radical about the learning experience: they tend to be more adaptable and flexible, and see opportunities for learning spaces differently from the orthodox view of a school as 'corridors and classrooms'.

The renowned Kunskapsskolan ('Knowledge School') architect, the late Kenneth Gärdestad, passionately pursued the belief that most of a school's internal area should be used for learning; that spaces should be open, transparent and actively promote collaborative working; and that there should be no corridors (typically some 30% of the gross internal area in many modern UK schools). These educational environments actively foster Kunskapsskolan's desired target- and step-based personalised learning and teaching styles, despite allowing a footprint of typically only 7–9m^2 per student (the minimum is 11m^2 per pupil in England and more in Scotland).

As Odd Eiken, Executive Vice-President of Kunskapsskolan (Sweden), explains:

> *Kunskapsskolan's schools are typically located in facilities which were originally built for other purposes … the architecture, characterised by light, visibility and flexibility, does not only allow for a more effective use of space; it also gives rise to an open and collaborative atmosphere. The starting point is not to divide space into static classrooms with connecting corridors, but to regard the entire space as a potential learning area.*[4]

Examples of buildings repurposed as Kunskapsskolan schools include:

- A former jewellery factory in Gothenburg
- A former textile factory in Landskrona (Figure 7.03)
- A disused submarine factory in Malmö – now a media school

The design of Vittra Telefonplan in an industrial area of Stockholm involved the conversion of

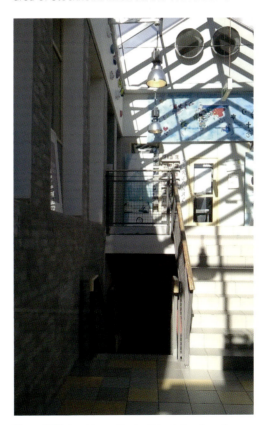

Figure 7.03 Landskrona Charter School, Sweden – A former textile factory

URBAN SCHOOLS: DESIGNING FOR HIGH DENSITY

Figure 7.04 Rosan Bosch Studio, Vittra Telefonplan, Stockholm, 2011 – Learning landscape

the former cabinetmaker's workshop in a former Ericsson telephone factory into a bilingual school without walls, creating innovative learning spaces through the use of bespoke furnishings to promote the learner-centric ethos and pedagogy.

In many cases, intervention into such buildings deliberately leaves their history plainly evident. The internal configuration of spaces is flexible, not constrained by load-bearing walls, services or building structure, so can be readily adapted if circumstances change.

According to Odd Eiken,

Visitors to Kunskapsskolan often remark that our schools look more like the site of a modern, creative knowledge industry rather than a traditional school. That may well be so, and, after all, isn't that the kind of working life the next generation needs to prepare for?[5]

Industrial buildings appear to lend themselves well to certain types of school use. The design of HGO (Heimdalsgades Overbygningsskole) in Copenhagen, Denmark, located in a former bread and paper factory, is organised around five 'competence environments' through which the pupils pass during their time at the school.

In the UK, University Technical Colleges for 14- to 19-year-olds have provided an interesting vehicle for repurposing industrial buildings. For example, Scott Brownrigg carried out an award winning conversion of the Grade II listed Great Western Railway Infant School, Great Western One and former Mill Building in the midst of railway sheds and train tracks in Swindon, Wiltshire, while Architect HKS designed the conversion of Grade II listed former marine and carpenters' workshops directly on the quayside in Newhaven, East Sussex to form UTC@Harbourside, which specialised in science, technology, engineering and mathematics (STEM). Notwithstanding the difficulties later encountered in making the UTC educational model viable, these examples demonstrate how conservation of a building of historic significance can be combined with contemporary design new-build to create a modern, industry-standard learning environment.

Strömberg School in Helsinki is a primary school converted from a redundant and poor-condition 1960s engineering training facility. Two separate buildings were internally remodelled and connected by a new main entrance hall. Floors were inserted in the former machine workshops. A multipurpose hall – the 'living room of the school' – has raked seating, an open fireplace and a small stage; a bridge crosses this space, connecting to a reading gallery and winter garden. Although part of the Helsinki school system, the school follows the unorthodox Freinet pedagogical model: mixed-age 'home' classrooms are smaller

Figure 7.05 Järvinen and Neimenen, Strömberg School, Helsinki, 2000

than normal classrooms and are arranged in fours with openable glass walls between pairs of rooms.

OPPORTUNITIES FOR RETAIL AND MIXED USE

Reuse of retail buildings as schools has been less common, partly because those large enough for a school tend to be both out-of-town developments away from the centre of population, and cheap 'shed' structures rather than substantial buildings. One particularly interesting example, however, is Highland Academy Charter School in Anchorage, Alaska. When it opened (as Highland Tech High), it was one of a US network of New Technology High Schools, a charter school with many freedoms due to its being outside local school board control. A member of Alaska's Re-Inventing Schools Coalition (RISC), the school operates a nontraditional competence-based curriculum based on proficiency in standards, making it the first standards-based school in Anchorage district.

The school is housed in a former Carrs-Safeway supermarket situated on a typical US strip mall at an intersection on Northern Lights Boulevard, Anchorage (with shops and car parking on all four corners of the crossroads). When it opened, all internal teaching, workshop, meeting and staff spaces were created with the simplest of timber partitions to a height of about 2.5m. Above them, the void of a typical 'tin shed' supermarket, with all ducting and structure, was left visible; the rationale for this was that one doesn't generally look above eye level if engaged with learning and other people. The beauty of this light-touch 'shopfitting' approach to internal spaces was that, after a few years, as the curriculum and teaching developed, so could the school adapt. Over one summer break, a team of tradesmen reconfigured the whole internal space and the students returned to a 'different' school after the vacation.

Conversely, the replacement of Tidemill Academy in Deptford, South-East London was seen as an opportunity for imaginative 'root and branch' regeneration of a tight urban site off the town centre high street, with sense of place as a guiding theme. With a rooftop play deck, the primary school sits within a community-building masterplan that includes 38 affordable dwellings, a community centre, art gallery, courtyard café, a state-of-the-art learning centre and library forming the 'Deptford Lounge', and a six-storey concrete frame building, the Resolution Studios, comprising nine high-quality incubation work studios for small local businesses. The steel frame building created for both public and school use encompasses a library on the ground floor, a gymnasium on the first floor and an Astroturf football pitch on the roof. Separate access points for the public realm ensure the security and safeguarding of the school pupils and staff. A biomass boiler, fuelled by sustainably-sourced wood pellets provides heating and hot water for the school and lounge, with a CHP (Combined Heat and Power) system heating the residential dwellings and studio units.

CHANGE OF USE: PRESERVING THE BUILDING'S ORIGIN

High-density redevelopment with multiple uses including education is an increasingly common

REUSE, REPURPOSE, SHARE

strategy for both optimising land use and contributing to urban regeneration, enabling community cohesion and creating opportunity. Queens Quay in Clydebank, East Dunbartonshire – once the site of the world-famous John Brown Engineering shipyard – now houses one of the three linked campuses of West College Scotland (formerly Clydebank College), offices, residential housing, a health centre, a care home, retail and business premises and public spaces alongside the River Clyde. Marking the site's historical roots, the massive iconic Titan crane has been refurbished as a landmark and visitor attraction.

Celebrating a site or building's history is a recurring thread. Sometimes this involves retaining artefacts which tell a story, and incorporating them in new-builds; in other cases, the building's provenance and former life are

Figure 7.06 PTE Architects, Tidemill Academy, Deptford, 2012

very evident in the form and architecture of the building, and are not disguised. For example:

- The Grade II listed fire station in Norwich now houses a free school, the Sir Isaac Newton Sixth Form (Architect: Pick Everard).
- The conversion of the 1930 Grade II listed Wormholt Library into the Ark Conway Primary Academy and Infant Welfare Centre, Acton, West London (Architect: Hunters South)

A building's history can create opportunity. Eden Girls' School, referenced earlier, transformed a redundant 1980s office block on a business park in Slough, the former BlackBerry HQ. The office building had the advantage of a business-like ethos and a sense of 'arrival': welcoming, with visibility and transparency and space for a generous reception area. Open-plan buildings such as this, without undue structural constraints, are easy to subdivide, but creating larger volumes requires more innovative interventions. By opening up the structure and removing floors, the architects created a full-height three-court sports hall within the building. Spatial inefficiencies allowed internal social spaces within corridors to be introduced, compensating for the limited site area. The five existing office staircases, whilst theoretically sufficient, were in the wrong places (the corners of the building), too narrow, and compromised student movement and orientation; the insertion of a new central grand staircase had a transformational effect, creating a primary circulation route and intuitive wayfinding. This intervention also allows daylight to penetrate deep into the heart of the three-storey plan and provides a canvas for a 14m-high graphic feature wall utilising words, phrases and concepts drawn from the school community's faith.

The new school building features a central staircase, a hub that buzzes with energy as pupils move between lessons. The breath-taking feature wall, measuring 100 square metres and adorned with the 99 divine attributes of Allah, is a stunning feature of our entrance hall to welcome visitors and inspire our pupils on a daily basis![6]

Examples exist of successful interventions into office buildings for temporary facilities. Trinity School, a secondary Christian free school in Sevenoaks, Kent leased a vacant office block in town and successfully operated in it for three years. Some external hard space was available, but the school also utilised local leisure facilities to meet curriculum needs. To avoid standard planning permission procedures, light-touch internal changes were completed in just four months under Permitted Development Rights.

An inventive office-based repurposing can also be found in Tothill Street, Central London. Harris Westminster Sixth Form (Architect: Nicholas Hare) – a collaboration between Harris Federation and the independent Westminster School – occupies a former Ministry of Justice high-rise building for the education of 250 academically able but socially disadvantaged young people. Unusual features are a seventh-floor canteen and assemblies being held in the church across the road and, occasionally, in Westminster Abbey.

Figure 7.07 Nicholas Hare Architects, Harris Westminster Sixth Form Academy, London

URBAN SCHOOLS: DESIGNING FOR HIGH DENSITY

Figure 7.08 Axonomic drawing of Nicholas Hare Architects' Harris Westminster School, Sixth Form Academy, London

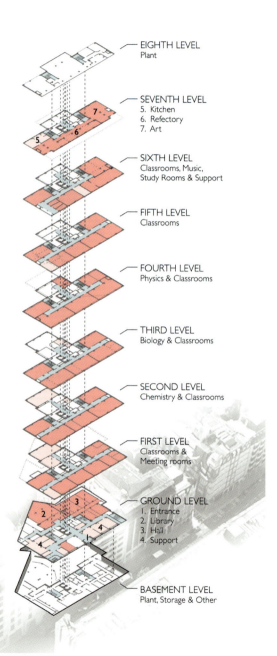

CONCLUSION

Place is where people, location and resources combine to create a sense of identity and purpose, and is at the heart of addressing the needs and realising the full potential of communities. Places are shaped by the way resources, services and assets are directed and used by the people who live in and invest in them.[7]

Innovation often occurs when, faced with a seemingly intractable problem, we are forced to think differently. The lack of urban sites where new schools are urgently needed has given rise to novel design solutions and inventiveness about schools' purposes, organisation and place in communities. Nationally and internationally we now see many pioneering examples of reused, repurposed, reimagined, shared, permanent and temporary buildings, not designed originally for educational purposes, now operating successfully as schools. These buildings challenge the traditional paradigm of what constitutes an effective learning environment. They present real opportunities but also new challenges for designers, contractors and the schools themselves. The boundaries of 'What is a school?' can be challenged further – for example, whether better value of the precious asset might be realised if school facilities were utilised ('owned') by other groups and activities at other times. Additionally, we might question whether schools need permanent premises or if 'pop-up schools' might better reflect changing demographics and education policy. All such considerations would be key to integrating schools fully and properly in their urban communities.

CHAPTER EIGHT

THE CONNECTED LEARNER

Ty Goddard

INTRODUCTION

If we truly see technology as an enabler of learning rather than just a tool for disseminating knowledge, we can better understand its potential. This shift allows us to fundamentally change how we think about individual, organisational and city-wide education opportunities. We can then question the spaces needed to support new modes of learning, and develop new ideas about how technology can support us in addressing the challenges of delivering in urban areas.

TEACH TO ONE

At Teach to One in New York (formerly the School of One), each student follows a completely individualised programme of learning – it is truly differentiated. This project, a standout from the era of the New York iZone project to connect and innovate among 250 NY schools, acknowledged from the outset that students may benefit by being taught mathematics in various different ways. Direct teacher instruction is blended with students' ability to access content through remote coaching – a form of digital top-up tuition. In the Teach to One programme, students are assigned different approaches based on expected skill level, and go on to participate in a variety of skill-building activities that include direct instruction from teachers, small group work with peers and online tutoring. Students are assessed daily to determine whether they have mastered a skill or need more time on that skill, with these assessments then used to determine what each student will work on the following class day.

With Teach to One, teachers are equipped with real-time data on student performance, and students learn only what they are ready for and do not move on to more advanced material until they have mastered a particular skill. This approach throws up a number of interesting issues around how technology can facilitate learning and consequent implications for the built environment. If we see students as individual learners, we move away from a classroom model of 30 children led by one adult, and perhaps our standard school spaces become less useful.

Instead, we need spaces which are more versatile and agile like the best workplaces, allowing students to work alone in a quiet area, to work in groups to develop skills and understanding, and to receive information from adults. The initial School of One programme employed a range of 'modalities' for learning: teacher-led, collaborative, virtual and independent instruction.[1]

We also see that technology acts as an enabler, not only allowing students to manage their own learning to an extent, but also allowing teachers to monitor and assess student progress in real time.

Teach to One tends to cater for smaller groups of students and so can be housed in spaces which would not be appropriate for our English secondary schools, where 600 students in four forms of entry may now be seen as too small to be economically feasible. A redundant school hall in New York was creatively refurbished to create environments for maths mastery. This was a purposeful pedagogy of space – and all in a high-school hall.

In Summer 2018, UK Education Secretary Damian Hinds recognised:

> *There is clear, untapped potential for schools, colleges and universities to benefit even further from the power of technology to support students to learn, reduce teachers' workload and save money.*[2]

Yet while the English government might slowly be coming to recognise the benefits of technology, it is still used within the other tight parameters of curriculum and funding for schools. Could technology yet be a driver for change in the UK as in the New York example? And could we think more deeply about spaces needed to support teaching and learning that happens to use technology?

Figure 8.01 School of One's Modalities

TEACHER-LED
Live Investigations

COLLABORATIVE
Small Group Collaboration

Peer-to-peer

VIRTUAL
Coached Virtual Instruction

Virtual Reinforcement

INDEPENDENT
Independent Live Practice

TASK SESSIONS

EDTECH AND SYSTEMIC CHANGE

Despite the introduction of the computing curriculum and a big dose of 'robot fever', there was for many years no real long-standing leadership for education technology; the establishment of various different task forces seemed to suggest a 'stop-start' mentality from government. Systemic change is hard, and in England we desperately need to restart the discussion at a national level to find out properly how education technology can make a meaningful contribution. We can learn much from Wales, Scotland and Northern Ireland about developing new approaches to the adoption of education technology. What's also striking is that there has been growing recognition from other parts of Whitehall that education technology (EdTech) is also important for the UK's economy, for jobs and exports. Most recently, in 2017, the UK Government's Digital Strategy stated: '[EdTech] is one of the fastest growing sectors in the UK, accounting for 4 per cent of digital companies, and UK businesses have become world leaders in developing innovative new technologies for schools.'[3] New announcements of a potential education technology strategy in January 2019 suggest a growing but above all active and welcome role for government across England, and in April 2019 the Department for Education announced an education technology strategy for England.

Progress, however, has been made in the use of EdTech by schools. There are also networks to support the adoption and understanding of EdTech by schools and colleges, but we need to embrace a broad vision and be alive to the possibilities that

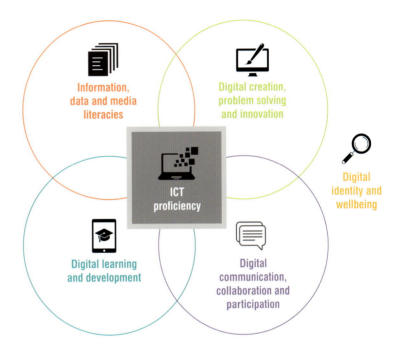

Figure 8.02 School of One's Principles

technology can bring to every aspect of school life. For too long we have ignored the fact that educational technology can rationalise the back office as much as enliven and focus learning and properly support the teacher. The work of the not-for-profit educational resource Jisc on 'digital capabilities' suggests the increasing importance of digital skills not only for study but to ensure students go on to thrive in the workplace.[4]

We know that investing in innovation, innovation brokers and educators to guide their peers reaps dividends – sharing practice and examples is key. The 'tyranny' of the perfect case study has never properly motivated anyone.

Educators respond to those sharing their own journeys with generosity and passion. The Education Foundation captures the learning of schools, colleges and universities in its annual *Edtech 50* publication, which shines a spotlight on those pioneering a new future in education through technology.

Among those included in the *Edtech 50* list is the leadership of Shireland Collegiate Academy in Smethwick. Sir Mark Grundy, who leads the Shireland Collegiate Academy Trust (Shireland CAT), is a pioneer of using education technology to support teaching and learning. Sir Mark is looking at broad change involving the whole school community and the creation of new tech-rich schools:

> *I have an incredible team and the trust of parents, students, Governors and staff. We have been harnessing the power of technology in education and transforming lives over many years. Moving into the primary phase is a natural step for us to ensure the skills are embedded younger and being used properly. I'm genuinely excited about the potential primary age children will have when they start secondary school with advanced technology skills.*[5]

Harnessing technology from class web platforms, data analytics and shared resources focuses teacher excellence and parent support for learning.

Universities are already doing this. For example, the University of Northampton's powerful vision of active blended learning has inspired discussions on the design of academic spaces to support students and educators. This has been given life in the university's new Waterside Campus, which encourages collaboration, discussion and, importantly, maximising usage of space.[6] Similarly, Southampton Solent University recently invested in the Spark, a teaching and learning building aimed at encouraging creative, interactive and flexible ways of learning. The Spark's central atrium and dramatic elevated 'pod' is offered for events and is deliberately visible to passers-by to create a stronger connection to the city.[7]

From vlogging teachers to student apps, online courses to an interactive book experience, schools, companies and technologists have provided pupils with new tools for learning, interacting and living – and importantly support teachers in combating workload challenges. Yet we have not fully explored what this means for the learning

Figure 8.03 A digital workshop at the RIBA *Disappear Here* exhibition with Rokesly Junior School

THE CONNECTED LEARNER

environment and how we might create spaces alongside this new technology rather than fit it into existing classrooms and labs. Can the world of work teach us anything?

THE DIGITAL CITY

Portsmouth College is another *Edtech 50* pioneer. Timetable reform and provision of an iPad to every student have improved the quality of the teaching experience and significantly increased the number of students applying to join the college. The innovations have helped to transform the students' experience of college life. The devices allow teachers to make lessons ever more interesting, up-to-date and engaging. Results and attendance have improved and there has been a significant growth in curriculum richness, while students are able to develop the independent research and digital literacy skills that are vital to their success at college and beyond. Principal Simon Barrable says,

> We're now starting to work across the city to share our expertise and what we've learnt with other schools. My vision is that Portsmouth becomes a digital learning city.

Exploring the idea of what a digital learning city might look like is an exciting possibility. If it is truly about questioning how we deliver education to maximise the benefits to the user and support the educator, we may well find that the traditional school estate no longer meets requirements. Instead, area-based initiatives may become more deeply embedded. Can we use our education assets in better ways across an area?

Figure 8.04 Scott Brownrigg, London Design Engineering UTC Newham, Robotics Lab

URBAN SCHOOLS: DESIGNING FOR HIGH DENSITY

Figure 8.05 Esa Ruskeepää Architects, Opinmäki Learning Centre, Espoo, 2015

In Espoo, Finland, the School as a Service (SaaS) operating model has been established. This innovative concept has been driven by the need for more flexible spaces and operating models to meet the needs for future learning. Rather than defining the school as a building, SaaS defines a school as a set of resources to support learning, in which the role of the learner, of all ages, is central. The SaaS experiment started in August 2016 when Haukilahti Upper Secondary School was relocated to premises on the Aalto University campus. Users were involved in design and implementation, and students have the added benefit of access to 50 university courses.

Further innovation is planned across the Espoo education system. For instance, a new metro line will make it easier for the students to move from one school to another and take in common courses.

And all of this is underpinned by technology to support innovation. Espoo has set up the

KYKY Accelerated Co-Creation programme, bringing together students, teachers, businesses and communities to allow EdTech businesses to implement and experiment with developing educational products and services inside the city's schools. Decisions are taken collaboratively between the schools and the companies; participating schools act as 'living labs' where students test new ideas and companies receive meaningful feedback on their products. Since the programme's launch in 2016, about 50 schools per year have signed up to be a part of the collaboration, which has increased digital skills among students and teachers. Each successful start-up company markets its products as being 'Co-Created with the City of Espoo Schools'. Co-creation is a key driver for ensuring ownership, understanding and implementation of these new ways of learning and working.

CONCLUSION

If we were to take as a starting point the lessons learned from our schools and universities that are leading on how to use technology to support learners and staff in schools, and then draw on some of the international innovation from the US and Finland, we could develop a system of schools around 'connected individuals'. That might allow us to set aside the notion that the building is always the initial starting point and focus instead on identifying the right clusters of learners, how technology can support new and innovative ways to support their learning, and what spaces are needed to enable them. It might be that students are not in the same place or same grouping every day, but technology could facilitate their staying connected. The education environment matters, and education technology adoption may mean it matters in new ways.

CHAPTER NINE

THE URBAN ENVIRONMENT FOR LEARNING

Dianne Western

INTRODUCTION

A study commissioned by Natural England in 2015 found that three-quarters of UK children spend less time outside than prison inmates, a fifth of the children did not play outside at all on an average day and 12% (around 1.3 million) rarely, if ever, visited the natural environment, including green spaces in towns and cities.[1] The pressure on development space and the consequent lack of green areas, an increasing focus on a digital world and a fear of crime and safety issues are contributing to a lack of contact with the outdoor world. Within this context, schools can play a key role in providing the opportunity for time outdoors and contact with the natural world.

What Richard Louv sets out in his book *Last Child in the Woods* (2005) has now become well known.[2] Rates of childhood obesity, attention deficit hyperactivity disorder, impaired social skills (including increasing violence) and mental health issues have increased to alarming levels.

A number of pieces of research have shown that spending time in nature can reduce blood pressure, anxiety, depression, stress, rumination and mental fatigue. Moreover, it can improve attention, memory, cognition, sleep, self-esteem and happiness.[3]

THE VALUE OF GOOD-QUALITY OUTDOOR SPACE

Children's early experiences lay down their foundations for learning, health and behaviour throughout life. If habits involving contact with nature are formed early, there is evidence that this lasts into later life, continuing to bring health and wellbeing benefits. School design should drive the incorporation and quality of outdoor space, as well as increasing the time that children are able or encouraged to spend in it. The importance of access to nature and play to cognitive development and learning is a well-established principle, supported through initiatives and charities such as Learning

Figure 9.01 Children feeding the swans at Tower Beach, River Thames, City of London, 1940

Through Landscapes, Forest Schools and Dirt is Good.

Research has established that exposure to green space can directly affect the cognitive ability of children.[4] It boosts their attention span and ability to focus, and improves creative thought processes and problem-solving abilities as well as mental control, self-discipline, and self-regulation.[5] However, contact with nature needs more than just didactic and curriculum-oriented activities: free play, exploration and child-initiated learning are more significant. Without contact with the natural world, children lose their ability to experience the world directly and to relate to others' life experience.[6]

Spending life indoors brings a risk of children losing their capacity to think or learn about the world directly, and is also now being considered as a source of stress and anxiety.[7]

The parents of children suffering from attention deficit hyperactivity disorder (ADHD) report that 85% of green space-related activities have a positive impact on their children's social interactions.[8] The positive effects of a greener and natural setting have also been proven to reduce ADHD symptoms.[9] In contrast, outdoor play on hard paved areas increases ADHD symptoms.[10] A study in the USA found that after a 20-minute walk through a park, children with ADHD had better concentration than those

THE URBAN ENVIRONMENT FOR LEARNING   95

Figure 9.02 Wynne-Williams Landscape Architects, Dulwich Hamlet Junior School

who had walked in an urban area. The study notes that 'green time', prescribed as part of the treatment of ADHD, is accessible, has no adverse side effects, and is non-stigmatising and inexpensive, if not free.[11]

These positive effects apply to any school. A study by the Department of Landscape Architecture, University of Illinois, demonstrated that placing children in classrooms with views to green landscapes has significant positive impacts on recovery from stress and mental fatigue.[12] When children become engaged in nature, their neural mechanisms can rest and recover. Without this, they will start to respond to distracting stimuli, lose concentration and find difficulty in managing daily tasks.[13]

CONNECTING SCHOOL CHILDREN TO THE NATURAL WORLD

Bringing nature into school and creating an integrated approach to the whole school environment is clearly going to be better than relying on break times alone. Green views can be orchestrated to include 'borrowed landscapes' – views of adjacent green space such as parks, green roofs, green walls or just street trees.

A US study of Austrian middle schools showed that refurbishment to increase vegetation levels helped reduce stress and enhance psychological wellbeing.[14] In Melbourne, students with a view of a green roof

Figure 9.03 Vignoles Gymnasium, Paris – Roof garden

made fewer errors and were able to concentrate better than those with views of concrete roofs.[15] Planting light shade trees near windows can provide a shield from hot summer sun, providing moving dappled shade in the breeze and letting in winter light though a tracery of branches.

A sense of openness is increasingly rare in a dense and claustrophobic urban location, and a chance to rest the eye is especially helpful after time looking at a screen, as well as in aiding creative thought. Moving clouds, rain on the window and changing weather are all ways to connect with nature, but the ability to see the sky, whether indoors or outside, is diminishing as the urban fabric grows taller. Alongside sun exposure, lack of light is a health issue – vitamin D deficiency in UK children tripled in the last four years.[16] Exposure to natural light affects mood and sleep patterns as well as immune suppression. The intensity of sunlight experience

THE URBAN ENVIRONMENT FOR LEARNING

Figure 9.04 Jane Drew Architect, Higher Secondary School, Sector 23, Chandigarh – Children climbing a concrete sun-screen

outside is far greater than through a window: on a clear summer day, light levels outside are 500 to 1,000 times greater than artificial lighting.

The principles of biophilic design are primarily aimed at internal spaces, but could equally apply to a hard landscape in a compact school, where each square metre needs to count.[17] The most effective designs involve direct experience of elements of nature – light, air, fire, water, weather, animals, plants, ecosystems and natural landscapes. Indirect experience through natural materials, patterns and colours is also helpful. The third way is through organisation of place and space – providing prospect and refuge, an enriched but organised environment with transitional spaces, particularly between indoors and outdoors, and clear wayfinding.

The creation of a verdant environment is a clear objective, but sterile exotic evergreens will have little effect. Planting needs to be in a natural style, emulating ecosystems as far as possible. With pressure on space, and the equally important need to provide areas to exercise and 'run free', external space needs to work hard. Green elements can be incorporated in vertical planes, with green walls, and in inaccessible areas such as roofs. Maximising sensory experience is key.

URBAN SCHOOLS: DESIGNING FOR HIGH DENSITY

The use of natural materials like wood and natural stone, sand, gravel or bark surfacing will also add to the character of the school environment. Maintenance and health and safety issues mean water can be difficult to incorporate in schools, but if it is possible, the best effects come from small moving elements of water that contain wildlife and involve natural patterns, sounds and light reflections.

AIR QUALITY AND COOLING

If much of our urban development is expected to last about 60 years, and if each site prioritises built form over existing trees, eventually very few mature trees will remain. As well as their

Figure 9.05 ANS Global, Hindhead Campus - an external living wall

Figure 9.06 NAC Architecture, Hazel Wolf K-8 E-STEM School, Seattle, 2017 – An internal living wall

myriad townscape character, biophilic and ecological benefits, trees – planted either within school grounds or adjacent in the public realm – can absorb pollutants and enhance air quality. More importantly, the reward from retaining existing trees within a redeveloped site far outweighs that of new planting. A 100-year-old tree has four times the cumulative benefits of a 50-year-old tree, and at 200 years, this reaches 20 to 40 times the benefits.[18] A large tree with a trunk diameter of 75cm can intercept ten times more air pollution and store up to 90 times more carbon than a tree of 15cm diameter, amounting to up to 24% reduction in particulate matter.[19] Retaining a mature tree is five times more cost-effective than periodic removal and replacement.[20] Trees can reduce temperatures by up to 2°C through shade and evapotranspiration, and green walls also improve air quality and cooling. A 1000m^2 section of an ivy wall is more efficient in absorbing carbon dioxide and producing oxygen than a mature beech tree with leaf surface of 1600m^2.[21] And children love them…

PROVIDING HIGH-QUALITY PLAY OPPORTUNITIES WITHOUT EXTENSIVE PLAYGROUNDS

With sufficient funds and time, challenging and interesting play opportunities in smaller spaces can be designed – but is 'play' enough?

Figure 9.07 Tezuka Architects, Fuji Kindergarten, 2007 – Retaining trees

Figure 9.08 Farrer Huxley Associates and Nicholas Hare Architects, Prior Weston Primary School, London – Rooftop play

Children's need to race around in some open space is clear to anybody passing a primary school playground, but contact with nature is a critical dimension that needs to be incorporated into a healthy environment.

Rooftop terraces can help extend the space available, but what facility is best accommodated at higher levels? To get a true hint of a natural environment, a little piece of wilderness, of dirt and freedom, there is a need to maximise use of the ground level for this, which implies sport is best located at higher levels.

This can bring its own challenges and issues, such as neighbour views, noise and maintenance, about which there needs to be an awareness and preparedness. For example, at the Prior Weston Primary School – part of the Golden Lane Campus in Barbican, London – the head teacher has concerns about the cost of regularly jet-washing the permeable

tarmac rooftop games court in order to keep it free-draining. Additional funds for this were not provided in the maintenance budget.

An alternative strategy could be to locate quieter spaces at higher levels, with growing areas, reading and more passive or reflective activities, perhaps even incorporating animal housing, as proposed for the redeveloped Barlby School, North Kensington. Incorporating the sports facilities at ground level in an imaginative and integrated manner is key to enabling a multifunctional role that does not obstruct other uses of the available space – perhaps by allowing 'free-flow' through staggered fencing rather than an entirely caged approach – and enabling peripheral space to have a purpose. Royal Greenwich Trust School provides an example in use: its two games courts are located centrally, with a peripheral training track incorporating multipurpose recreation space.

ACTIVITY AND FITNESS

In dense urban areas play space can be sparse. Opening school facilities out of hours must be a way to help address this. Multigenerational play may help address security concerns, as well

Figure 9.09 The Landscape Partnership, working with Walters and Cohen Architects, Royal Greenwich Trust School (formerly Royal Greenwich UTC) – Games courts are placed centrally, with peripheral activities

URBAN SCHOOLS: DESIGNING FOR HIGH DENSITY

Figure 9.10 The Landscape Partnership, Royal Greenwich Trust School – A peripheral training track with distance markers provides motivation for fitness activity

as having wider health benefits: studies show that adults and children who exercise and play outdoors are active more often and for longer periods of time, and 75% of children prefer outdoor play with parents or grandparents over video games.[22]

An element of challenge and risk within play is encouraged by authorities and professionals involved in childcare and education. Not only does physical challenge aid children to gain strength and coordination and to grow and develop cognitive skills, but experiencing controllable risk can aid motivation, memory, problem solving and fight-or-flight responses, as well as developing risk assessment during childhood.[23] It has also been suggested that experiencing confrontations, threats and physical challenges in an outdoor environment can increase energy levels and confidence.[24]

ADDRESSING BARRIERS TO OUTDOOR LEARNING

Once fantastic school grounds are created, there still needs to be motivation and commitment from the school, starting with the head teacher and including teaching and maintenance staff, to make use of the opportunity to spend time and learn outdoors. This is often recognised at primary school, with varying approaches and degrees of enthusiasm, but at secondary level it frequently depends on there being time allowed in the curriculum. The effort and time taken to escort a class of students outside can seem disruptive and inefficient, but how much of this is due to a lack of appreciation and understanding of how much benefit could be realised? Ideally the curriculum would require and provide for this aspect of learning, but even without this, useful convenient external facilities and a creative and imaginative approach to teaching and learning can make a difference.

The danger of mud being tracked into the building can lead to pristine playgrounds that are at best like corporate hotels or offices, and at worst like car parks. However, there are simple, and perhaps old-fashioned, ways of managing this, like having outdoor and indoor footwear. Furthermore, evidence shows that contact with dirt, rather than being detrimental, can boost the immune system.[25]

OUTDOOR PLAY

'Physical literacy' is the term applied to the basic movement skills that children usually acquire through early childhood, leading to confidence and competence, and boosting health and wellbeing (physical, mental, social and emotional). There is growing evidence that some children starting school lack basic balance, coordination and agility skills, as well as advanced skills such as catching and striking objects.[26] Stimulating playgrounds can provide subtle and appealing ways of encouraging this development, and the availability of a suitable range of facilities directly affects activity levels at break by up to three times.[27]

However, at secondary school level there is not much information available. From discussions about secondary school play, the Scottish division of Learning through Landscapes (LtL) (formerly known as Grounds for Learning) reports that the average Scottish secondary at a break or lunch can be an uninspiring experience:

> 'Playgrounds' are often of the bleak tarmac variety. They feature large open spaces with wind whistling through, with a few seats scattered around, laid out to look good on an architect's plan or to save some budget at the end of a build. In many, the choice of being outside is rejected, and legions sit on stairs indoors, interacting with others via social media.[28]

LtL Scotland notes that play for 11- to 18-year-old students is limited by the many rules and peer social codes, with minimal engagement and boredom prevalent. It is critical of the apparent abandonment of design principles upheld for primary school design once the magic line is crossed at age 11, and observes adolescents tend to be searching for identity, experience and meaning, requiring adults to consider what 'play' means for them and to adjust our thinking accordingly. We need to ensure we provide environments that allow teenagers to experiment with social play, enjoy mastering physical or purposeful activity and maintain their connection with nature, allowing them to benefit (particularly when under exam pressure) from the de-stressing and restorative qualities of pleasant green space.[29]

The lack of spaces to play – due both to non-stimulating environments and the decrease in available space – is partly to blame for the drop in physical activity at break times. In England, implementation of the Basic Need funding policy is leading to diminished playground sizes, with break times becoming shorter and attention often absorbed by online activity.

ACHIEVING WELL-DESIGNED OUTDOOR SPACES

The factors affecting the quality of high-density school external environments and the successful use of the outdoors are wide-ranging and occur at various phases of school design.

(a) Design Drivers and Brief

At the heart of the design process is the brief – both the general government requirements for schools and the specific project brief. The current ESFA templates for design briefs make little reference to the quality of external areas, however, and although there is mention in the General Design Brief (under the heading of habitat areas) of the requirement to provide suitable outdoor spaces 'to provide various teaching and learning resources across the whole curriculum in accordance with any areas identified in the SSB', in practice the Specific School Briefs rarely take up the opportunity. In reality, there is typically little time or attention allocated in a design process to the quality of external areas, and their quantity is under increasing pressure. It takes a highly motivated 'champion', usually a head teacher, to drive the brief and design agenda into spending time and budget on this aspect of a school. In the current design process, there are rarely any technical specialists in landscape design on the 'client' advisor team, often leaving the planning authority (if they have the relevant expertise) providing the only spotlight on the external areas.

Even if a brief does refer to outdoor learning, there is little perceived time available in the curriculum to take pupils outside to learn. For new schools there may be no experience on the client team of the benefits of good-quality external spaces. Yet once schools have this type of facility, they usually recognise its value and would elect to prioritise this in future situations.

Special Educational Needs schools require a particular and attentive approach to external area design. Detailed input is often required to the design brief, through dialogue and workshops, as each school tends to have different requirements, sometimes changing from one year to another, depending on specific pupil needs. There is not always sufficient time to develop thinking, and for new schools a head may not yet be appointed. Therefore, a specialist able to understand both the pupil and school requirements – and technical opportunities and constraints – is valuable in supporting the brief development.

(b) Design and Planning Process

Engagement by the client team in the landscape design process is always better where primary schools are concerned, but at secondary level this element can often be neglected or disregarded. Landscape architects are not always appointed on the team, or may not have suitable influence in the design process.

The early involvement of landscape architects in site planning is key to achieving the

THE URBAN ENVIRONMENT FOR LEARNING

foundations for the best external environment. Priority given to tree retention is an example of how wider benefits can be provided; this can make an enormous difference to both the school and the surrounding area, as well as smoothing the path of a planning application.

Unsurprisingly, the more environmentally sensitive sites will attract the most attention in relation to the quality of the landscape. It is perhaps ironic that, though the most challenging places for a school development, sensitive sites may yield the best external environments. The additional scrutiny (as part of the planning process) of the Planning Authority and statutory consultees – such as Sport England, English Heritage, Local Wildlife Trusts, Design Review Panels, Greater London Authority and the Environment Agency – will usually lead to

Figure 9.11 Macgregor Smith Landscape Architects and Dixon Jones Architects, Marlborough Primary School, London, 2018 – Roofscape

Figure 9.12 McGregor Smith Landscape Architects and Dixon Jones Architects, Marlborough Primary School, London, 2018 – Play space

an enhanced quality compared with a more standard site.

The requirements of the Building Research Establishment Environmental Assessment Method (BREEAM) can also drive aspects of the green space agenda, although some criteria are hard to apply to small sites as they require multiple species and areas. However, since landscape and ecology credits are relatively highly weighted and cost-effective to achieve, they provide one of the few drivers for landscape design. The latest version of BREEAM (2018) favours ecology credits for genuine natural habitats such as 'woodland' and wildflower meadows, which are impractical on a small urban site. However, preservation of existing natural features or improvements to brownfield sites will achieve better scores.

THE URBAN ENVIRONMENT FOR LEARNING

Figure 9.13 Haverstock, The Belham Primary School, Southwark

(c) Cost and Priorities

It is well known that landscape design is often one of the last items to be confirmed and the first to be cut when a 'Value Engineering' exercise is required. Budget pressures apply to design fees and services as well as to the construction budget. Professional landscape architects are not always engaged, which can mean there is nobody suitably qualified to justify and explain the needs and benefits of the landscape design at critical moments, or to ensure it is executed satisfactorily.

An enriched design will often be seen as complex and expensive compared with plain asphalt and simple shapes. Intensive green roofs can be 'dumbed-down' or omitted after tenders are returned. These roofs must be irrigated to survive, yet some BREEAM credits will not be achieved if any irrigation is installed. Trees are also seen as an easy target for budget reduction, being obvious to count and perceived as costly. Yet, increasingly, commercial developers are retaining good-quality landscape design and appreciate trees within their proposals, as they have a demonstrable asset value to the development.

One of the factors affecting the cost of installing trees in compact urban projects is the need to provide adequate and suitable rooting space to enable them to establish and flourish, achieving the maximum benefits they are planted for. Root cells that allow hard paved areas to be constructed successfully over these underground volumes can significantly add to cost. But these, too, can work hard, providing additional flood attenuation, and the importance of trees in air quality and urban cooling cannot be underestimated. Greater recognition is needed that, comparatively, trees are a low-cost, high-impact element with multiple benefits.

The final, but by no means least important, design hurdle is the necessity to budget and plan for maintenance, and to design for minimal maintenance. This will allow the landscape proposals to reach their full potential, enabling them to be appreciated, used and valued. A neglected feature will soon be removed altogether, an action regarded as the simplest and cheapest solution.

(d) Understanding the Opportunity

Even if a head teacher is involved at the design stage, this does not necessarily mean that

108   URBAN SCHOOLS: DESIGNING FOR HIGH DENSITY

Figure 9.14 Ecole élémentaire Charles Hermite, and Ecole 70 Avenue Daumesnil, Paris, where the Paris Oasis Schools Project (a partnership with 100 Resilient Cities) aims to transform schoolyards into urban cooling islands, benefiting the local area, by increasing vegetation and replacing asphalt with porous surfacing

THE URBAN ENVIRONMENT FOR LEARNING

Figure 9.15 Katy Staton Landscape Architecture and David Morley Architects, Kings Cross Academy and Frank Barnes School for Deaf Children, London, 2015 – Play decks

outdoor opportunities will fully be understood and passed on. Teaching staff are not usually involved in the current streamlined design process and may not have the experience or training to know how to best use the resources. The employment of key staff who have some expertise in these areas and training around outdoor learning is obviously going to be most helpful. Contact or handover with teaching staff is crucial; this might include a list of advisory contacts, and a document illustrating opportunities provided by the external areas. Template guidelines or advice for schools provided by the funder, perhaps as part of the technical output, could make a difference even if no additional budget is available.

Scotland's government is progressing embedding outdoor learning into the curriculum. In 2013 it accepted the 'One Planet Schools' recommendations produced the previous year by WWF Scotland, which proposed that outdoor learning should be a regular, progressive curriculum-led experience for all learners.[30] This concept combines sustainable development, global citizenship and outdoor learning to help deliver key priorities in education, including raising attainment and improving behaviour, inclusion and health and wellbeing.

Consequently, Scottish Government policy states that children should encounter nature in their school grounds on a daily basis, while the 'Learning for Sustainability' agenda of the Curriculum for Excellence aims to ensure that progressive and sustainable outdoor learning opportunities are embedded in the curriculum. It includes addressing the issue of suitably trained staff. One of the questions posed in Education Scotland's school self-evaluation guidance *How Good is Our School?* is: 'Have teachers experienced continuing professional development (CPD) addressing outdoor/first-hand learning & teaching?' Scottish schools can also expect to be inspected on their approaches to learning for sustainability and outdoor learning.

CONCLUSION

There is growing public awareness of the importance of the outdoors, especially with regard to health and wellbeing, environmental stewardship and climate change. However, there is still much to do at government policy level in terms of the need to understand the wider value of good-quality outdoor learning spaces. We need joined-up thinking in relation to education, health and climate change budgets, and to ensure the longer-term objectives are embedded in policy and not usurped by cyclical challenges of time and budget.

Even without a much-needed increase in allowances for landscape installation and maintenance, a re-established commitment to good-quality environments and outdoor learning in all schools for all ages would be a positive outcome.

Our schools can provide green sanctuaries, air quality improvements, cooling and community facilities; they can create improvements in social cohesion, health and wellbeing, as well as education. Adjacent development and public realm must be viewed in tandem, returning benefits for schools – a multifunctional approach to development.

THE URBAN ENVIRONMENT FOR LEARNING | 111

Figure 9.16 The Landscape Partnership, working with Alsop Architects, Michael Faraday School, Southwark – Simple, cost-effective natural areas

Figure 9.17 David Morley Architects, Kings Cross Academy and Frank Barnes School for Deaf Children, London, 2015 – Both the school and the public benefit

CHAPTER TEN
BUILDING SCHOOLS IN URBAN ENVIRONMENTS

Helen Taylor

INTRODUCTION

The logistics and challenges around constructing schools in tight urban environments has as much to do with political drivers and funding requirements as it does with physical constraints. Schools in cities worldwide are being built in locations deemed unsuitable in the past. The shortage of available land, plus the acceptance that old office and industrial buildings can be converted for school use, has created a new set of technical challenges. Fitting the 'standard' schedule of accommodation on a small footprint will necessitate a taller building, or closer proximity to or integration with other activities such as residential and retail development. These new constraints create unusual design and construction challenges.

The school becomes a part of the city, and the relationship between the school and the public realm is a key element of success. The typical external envelope, material finishes, fenestration and transparency needs to adjust – sometimes radically – to the needs of the city surroundings. These are not just design and construction challenges, but operational and maintenance challenges (and costs) to be borne for the life of the school. In a time when children's health and wellbeing is a cause for concern throughout the world, meeting these technical challenges is vital to create positive, healthy, integrated spaces for education in the city.

Accommodating children in spaces visible to the street or above ground demands particular attention. Play, circulation and safe escape are the common concerns. The typical conversation about the quality of the internal space for education can become lost when focus shifts to the practical functionality and architectural form.

This chapter maps the design and operational challenges against the globally recognised RIBA Plan of Work for projects.

URBAN SCHOOLS: DESIGNING FOR HIGH DENSITY

RIBA STAGE 0–1: INCEPTION TO FEASIBILITY

Every single school is different, but in cities there is an even greater need for a site-specific approach from the outset. This starts from the need for an extended team of specialists and extensive site investigations: Party Wall and Right to Light Surveyors for dealing with tight boundary issues; magnetometer surveys to detect the presence of unexploded bombs or landmines; transport assessments to assist with the development of any travel plans, and to detail underground railway lines or other major infrastructure or utilities in close proximity to, or beneath, the site. Heritage and/or specialist planning or zoning consultants, stakeholder engagement or political consultants can be vital where the requirements and drivers of a local development authority, the school, the funder and of course the neighbours may be in conflict.

Building within a constrained urban site typically means constructing over a previous building or land use, and in some cases archaeological remains, which may add time and cost to the programme. If there are existing buildings to be demolished or refurbished, this will necessitate other surveys such as building and structural, asbestos, utilities, ground investigation and CCTV for drainage. The need

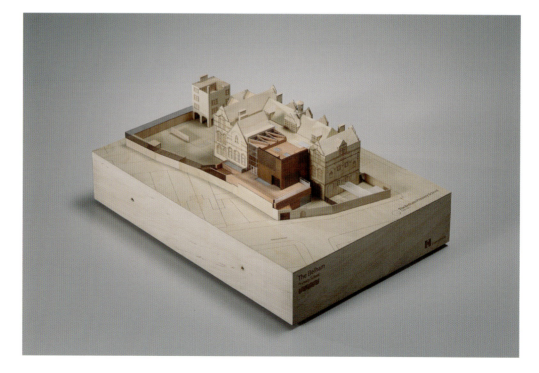

Figure 10.01 Haverstock, Belham Primary School, London, 2018 – Physical model

for dealing with contamination, or relocation of services and drainage, is one that most city developments are used to.

Air pollution is an issue that many are clamouring for governments to solve rather than schools to mitigate. Many inner-city schools are located where air pollution exceeds the legal limit of nitrogen dioxide, primarily due to vehicle traffic. The noise and vibration from traffic, and also from rail or aircraft, also has an impact. The outcome of air quality and acoustic surveys may have a significant bearing on the ventilation approach adopted for the project: a mechanically ventilated building may be the obvious choice, but entails both additional capital cost and running cost for the school.

> *Outdoor NO_2 concentrations and the airtightness of the building envelope explained 84% of the NO_2 variation between classrooms, indicating the influence of strong outdoor pollution sources and the importance of the building envelope*[1]

However, there is evidence that air quality and temperature control within sealed environments is no better than outside (and is sometimes worse).[2] Noise generated by activities and service installations on the school itself must also be managed; this can drive design strategies that add cost to the project and constrain future use of the facilities. Primary schools

Figure 10.02 Wynne Williams Associates, Robert Browning Primary School – Rooftop play

URBAN SCHOOLS: DESIGNING FOR HIGH DENSITY

Figure 10.03 Perkins + Will Architects, William Jones College Prep, Chicago, 2013 – Street frontage

discussion, investigation and decision-making. The school community may be discouraged from reliance on cars as a means of getting to and from the school. An assessment needs to be carried out at an early stage as it will likely impact on space requirements for car and cycle parking, as well as potential financial contributions to transport infrastructure improvements. The age and number of pupils, plus local cultural norms, make an enormous difference to how this challenge is dealt with in cities around the world; even in a car-free development there is likely to be some ongoing vehicle access depending on the age range and mobility of pupils, as well as for servicing needs and for transporting pupils to off-site sports facilities or school trips. Holding points away from the main school, or staggered starts, can solve space restrictions. Red routes, bus routes, parking restrictions, one-way access and adjacent buildings, pavements, pedestrian crossings, barriers and road markings all become part of the school's area of concern. Schools are great at solving problems, but the resources they need to manage unusual situations and solutions must be acknowledged.

RIBA STAGE 2–5: CONCEPT DESIGN TO CONSTRUCTION

Constructing a tall building requires a competent contractor, but schools can struggle to access equally competent resources to operate and maintain elements included in these buildings such as rooftop plant or play terraces. This influences roof access, maintenance, perimeter protection and both interior and exterior cleaning strategies, and affects capital and operational budgets.

sometimes have to battle to locate hard play on a roof space because of noise concern from neighbours.[3]

Although one of the great benefits of a city-centre school is access to public transport, the issue of traffic also generates significant

BUILDING SCHOOLS IN URBAN ENVIRONMENTS   117

CASE STUDY: Harris Invictus Academy, Croydon – Inception to handover

Harris Invictus Academy in West Croydon, London moved into its new high street premises in 2018. The project was conceived by Invictus, a grassroots community organisation, working in partnership with the Harris Federation (a Multi Academy Trust) with the aim of meeting significant demand within the community for new high-quality school places for local children.

The new school for 1,150 pupils occupies the constrained, inner-city site of a former hospital in an area that suffered from an extremely poor urban environment. This busy high street and major route into central Croydon suffered extensive damage in the 2012 riots, which led to Croydon Council prioritising the comprehensive regeneration of the area.

The project was procured through the Government ESFA Contractors Framework, and subject to the standard Schedule of Accommodation, Output Specification and funding envelope. Croydon planners' high aspirations for a landmark building to act as a catalyst for urban regeneration were at odds with the ESFA's standard modus operandi and budget. Collaboration was key.

The building has been positioned on the site boundary, forming the secure line and reinforcing the school's community-facing presence and focal point within the area. The building has been articulated as three distinct elements through materiality, transparency and use. Spaces utilised by pupils and the community have been placed at ground floor to provide an active frontage at street level. In the evening the building is transformed: internally lit glazed spaces become fully visible to the community, and the building acts as a beacon in the neighbourhood. There is a sense of pride in the school amongst local people. As Chris Randall of Harris Federation notes, 'the building's presence and impact seeing it from London Road fulfils the challenging brief perfectly'.

The building is utilised well beyond the typical seven-hour school day, an aspiration identified early in the client briefing process. To make this financially sustainable, a Combined Heat and Power plant was provided to lower

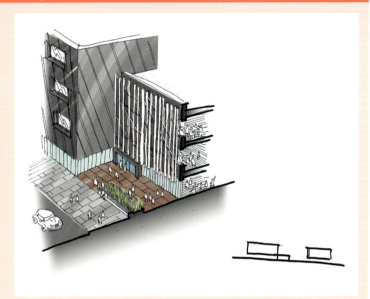

Figure 10.04 Scott Brownrigg, Harris Invictus, Croydon, 2018 – Concept sketch

Figure 10.05 Galliford Try, Harris Invictus, Croydon, 2018 – Community engagement

URBAN SCHOOLS: DESIGNING FOR HIGH DENSITY

CASE STUDY: Harris Invictus Academy, Croydon – Inception to handover (*CONTINUED*)

Figure 10.06 Scott Brownrigg, Harris Invictus, Croydon, 2018 – Neighbourhood beacon

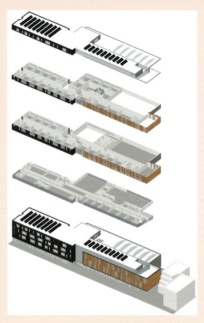

Figure 10.07 Scott Brownrigg, Harris Invictus, Croydon, 2018 – Stacked accommodation

energy use by optimising consumption and thereby decreasing carbon emissions alongside operational costs.

The school is arranged over four floors, with generous circulation and key adjacencies between subjects to alleviate the pressures associated with pupil movement. Good levels of natural light, natural ventilation, effective acoustic design, passive supervision and an emphasis on modern technology in the teaching spaces contribute to student attainment. The new building provides inspirational settings for teaching and learning along with opportunities for enterprise and community engagement. The oversubscribed school is ranked 'Outstanding' by Ofsted.

The choice of materials for the front elevation reinforces the three elements of the building concept, while the rear elevation responds to the residential context. The industrial aesthetic of the interior design mirrors the urban context and provides robust and durable finishes. The high thermal mass properties of the exposed concrete and blockwork also significantly reduce energy use.

The public realm outside the school has been reimagined to provide a generous open space with high-quality material finishes that tie into a local network of public spaces, alleviating pressure on the existing pavements. Building upwards to minimise the building footprint allowed external recreational space

to be maximised, a key strategic move which ensured that a floodlit multi-use games area could be provided. Students enjoy this facility during the day, and by evening and at weekends it has become a popular community destination.

The school had a number of challenges to consider during the construction phase, predominantly the very constrained site. Access was only via the surrounding residential streets as stopping on the busy London Road was prohibited. The school operated in temporary accommodation at the rear of the site throughout the construction period, further

BUILDING SCHOOLS IN URBAN ENVIRONMENTS   119

CASE STUDY: Harris Invictus Academy, Croydon – Inception to handover (*CONTINUED*)

constraining the site and compound. Close liaison with the school and consideration of its operations was vital to ensure education continuity, effective disruption management, segregation and safeguarding, and the health, safety and welfare of pupils, staff and users of the school site. Even during the construction period, the school still managed to achieve Ofsted 'Outstanding' status.

Figure 10.08 Scott Brownrigg, Harris Invictus, Croydon, 2018 – Restrained materials and transparency

Figure 10.09 Scott Brownrigg, Harris Invictus, Croydon 2018 – Robust urban context and materials

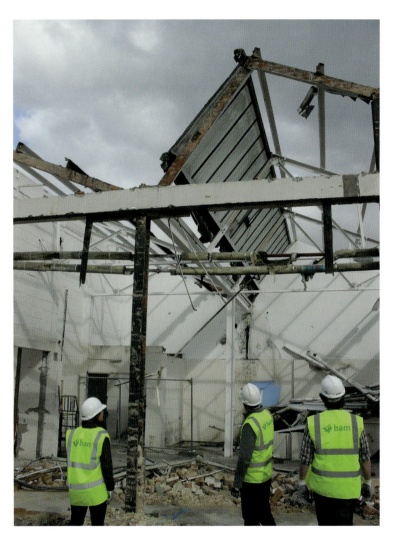

Figure 10.10 Walters & Cohen, Royal Greenwich UTC, London 2013 – BAM Construction examine the exposed frame

Self-cleaning glass and integrated maintenance cradles are not commonly found in schools. In the UK the Construction Design and Management (CDM) Regulations drive health & safety in design, construction and operation, but ultimate legal responsibility lies with the client as the leader of the project. The complex layers of stakeholders in a school project can make this responsibility unclear in the decision-making process; the funder and the operator may not both be involved in the building at the same time and schools may have to take on the operation of buildings that they had little say in designing.

The balance between a positive, usually glazed, urban street frontage that engages with its surroundings and the safeguarding and privacy of pupils requires consideration. Additional space may be required internally to replace the usual safe 'buffer zone' of a playground. Emergency escape takes on a different emphasis when the occupants are large groups of children: the population of a school is not always able to move fast or unaided, and inclusive access and escape need to be fully considered so all pupils can access the entire curriculum. Fire safety, means of escape, refuges, compartmentation, sprinklers, evacuation strategies, muster points and firefighting access may drive the design solution and must remain key drivers from inception to completion and into operation. The tragic Grenfell Tower fire in London in June 2017 has brought the issue of fire-safe construction and safe evacuation into sharp relief.

Schools may have to rethink timetables, providing longer lessons with less movement or having teachers move instead of students. More storeys means increased travel time and requires greater consideration and allocation of 'non-net' areas such as circulation, toilets and plant rooms or risers. There is a danger that the smaller the footprint, the greater the percentage of each floorplate given over to these non-net areas, making it difficult to organise the learning accommodation in an effective way. The usage,

BUILDING SCHOOLS IN URBAN ENVIRONMENTS   121

Figure 10.11 Perkins + Will Architects, William Jones College Prep, Chicago, 2013 – A typical classroom with opening window

number and type of lifts may be a challenging subject but the brief for stairs should be simple: they are vertical corridors, important spaces used for a large proportion of the day that need to be part of the learning environment and that offer a great opportunity to orientate and regularly connect pupils with their city surroundings through natural light and views.

Certain 'natural' adjacencies may not be possible with restricted floorplates. This impacts on service routes and the overall extent of space required for services, storage and support. For example, if laboratories are on different floors, it may require an additional Science Prep room with a secure holding area allowing science technicians to safely transport and store chemicals and equipment between lessons. Deliveries, kitchens and dining opportunities have the same challenge. Core support provision such as staff bases and accessible toilets need to be replicated on every floor, and access to the outside becomes something needed on more than just the street level. All these challenges require duplicated or additional spaces. A 'typical' space allocation based on pupil numbers will not deliver the same distribution of accommodation in a multi-storey school as in the low-rise school it was written for. A combined facility, stacked with residential or commercial accommodation, may have structure, environment, circulation and escape needs that are different from those of the function it is co-located with. If this is not addressed at the outset, the typical overall area allowance will struggle to meet the need.

Competition for the ground floor, fierce in every school, is compounded where space is tight. In multi-storey urban schools, competition for the roof space is similarly fierce: a battle between plant space and external teaching or social space, hard usable surfaces and green roofs. Priorities need to be established and maintained to ensure that the learning environment takes priority, particularly where ground-level space may be taken up with provisions outside the control of the project team – for example a new substation, fire vehicle access, or underground infrastructure protections. When construction has to accommodate a school in occupation on the site, this can have a fundamental impact on the design outcome. Any phased handover provides an additional complication and schools need to be realistic about what this means for them in terms of space for learning during construction.

The potential form, materials and construction method are restricted in a tight site. Tight urban sites may lend themselves to increased modular or off-site modern methods of construction, although modules still need to be transported and installed, which might involve closing parking bays or roads, or significant use of large cranes. Materials or components may have to be produced in smaller sections to enable them to be transported into the site. The phasing and accessibility of a constrained site will have an impact on costs and logistical arrangements, such as requiring additional craneage where offloading of materials needs to be accelerated due to a lack of space for delivery vehicles. Some developments may require partial possession of the school to meet curriculum dates. On mixed development sites, there may be a delay in possession due to non-school related construction issues such as construction being carried out above or the servicing and commissioning of shared plant. The contractor's site accommodation may have to move or not actually be on the site at all. Constant communication is key.

RIBA Stage 6+: Handover and Operation

Schools have to stretch the usual resources to manage unusual facilities. School buildings should be designed to facilitate operation and minimise operational costs. As illustrated in Chapter 3, the curriculum needs of schools change over time, and the constraints of buildings themselves can force a change in ways of working and expectations of behaviour. The desire for functional adjacencies to manage timetabling may be at odds with a layout that supports the building's energy efficiency or technical performance. The impact of daily movement on space dedicated to circulation and the need for moving parts such as elevators puts unusual pressure on school management.

At a strategic level, as noted in Chapter 4, there is a close interrelationship between building design, operation, staffing, pupil numbers and group sizes. But detail also really matters. Children need an environment that is engaging and experiences that will spark their imaginations. Unfortunately, concerns about safeguarding sometimes overwhelm the opportunity to do something different, particularly in these times of heightened security measures.

If you try to design for every eventuality, do you end up not really meeting any needs? Multipurpose spaces are difficult to get right. As Chapter 5 explores, how do you design an internal space that meets both school and community needs? How do you secure priority for education over housing need (or vice versa) in a mixed-use development? A supermarket under a school, as in the Deer Park School example currently under construction, is challenging the supermarket Lidl's standard approach to installing plant and services. All building occupants need to adjust and make compromises.

The provision of complex adjacencies in stacked environments is both a technical building and operational challenge. Timetabling is a complex process and every school building in a city requires innovation. Managing noise, managing air pollution, managing pedestrians and vehicles all need site-specific solutions. In mixed-use environments, holistic energy strategies need to be considered alongside issues of overshadowing, daylight, orientation and hours of use that create complex problems to solve. The value and ownership of the various spaces can skew the power in the process.

However Chapter 7 illustrates that it's not just about having the money or the power. The fabric and services in existing buildings may inherently preclude some solutions. Predetermined elements such as the structural frame, materials, site layout or floor to ceiling heights can create rigid constraints that necessitate innovative approaches to design and operation. Although it might be the most appropriate solution, the reuse of an existing building is not always a cheaper solution in the short or long term. Lifecycle, renewal and maintenance, material and energy use all need to be considered holistically. When the solution requires extreme remodelling, as at Eden Girls' School, the benefits of reuse are less clear. If Trinity School in Kent can operate successfully for three years in a leased office block, why are such radical changes necessary? The refurbishment of Harris Westminster Sixth Form Academy from a former Ministry of Justice office reveals the common driver for change:

> *The awkward existing arrangement of space at the lower levels, with deep floorplates and limited access to daylight, set a challenge that required innovative solutions in order to transform it into an uplifting education environment.*[4]

Where existing buildings have been successfully repurposed, it is often where a school's curriculum and modes of learning allow a more flexible approach. The nontraditional curriculum of the Highland Academy Charter School, Alaska, for example, can support a more easily reconfigured 'loose fit' layout, less focused on achieving a standardised specification for technical performance and more easily facilitating change. The Helsinki school examples illustrated in Chapter 7 celebrated the character of their repurposed buildings – they are deliberately different. Learning approaches can and do change depending on the physical environments where they are undertaken.

Figure 10.12 Landskrona Charter School, Sweden – A former textile factory

Chapter 7 suggests 'pop-up schools' in shared environments might provide better value for money, but the combined integrated management required to deliver and operate this approach has not produced many examples. The School as a Service model in Finland, for instance, can rely on children's ability to travel independently because of a well-connected and dependable public transport system.

However, our quickly evolving digital infrastructure is starting to facilitate a more flexible and responsive approach to meeting learner needs. Certainly the individualised learning at Teach to One in New York, illustrated in Chapter 8, is completely reliant on access to a digital learning environment, although also facilitated by a 'walls down' open-plan classroom space for team teaching. The 'implementation guide' generated by the study programme at what was then known as School of One clearly illustrated that the physical space was as instrumental in the success of the programme as teacher aptitude. Acoustics, finishes and furniture, flexibility and travel distance all matter, as the guide emphatically stated: '*Space plays a critical role in the implementation of the School of One.*'[5]

The versatility and agility of open-plan workspaces emulated in this approach needs investment and ownership, but we do not yet understand the impact of digital learning on school space. Moreover, the needs keep changing. Are we building flexible enough environments? How should we be building to enable the vision of the principal of Portsmouth College to create a 'digital learning city'?

In the excitement of a digital future, too, we must not neglect some fundamental needs. In Chapter 9, Dianne Western reminds us that regular access to the natural world has positive impacts on child development and behaviour. Trees and plants are a vital part of the urban infrastructure, and can help moderate temperature and air quality. The technical challenges of building and maintaining successful external environments for schools can be let down by a lack of detail in the brief or lack of expertise on the team. Feeling the wind on your face should be a sensory experience, not a battle against the elements in an urban wind tunnel. But movement is also vital. In Denmark this requirement has been law since 2013. Frederiksbjerg School in Aarhus was the first new school building to integrate this legal requirement into the design, prioritising 'learning through movement and sensation as well as openness and community creation. Part of the reform is a demand of a minimum of 45 minutes of movement and activity throughout school hours.'[6] 'The facilities … seek to incorporate sport every day in school activities.

BUILDING SCHOOLS IN URBAN ENVIRONMENTS | 125

Everywhere in the complex there are places for gymnastics, climbing, running and jumping'.[7]

CONCLUSION

A building is not an object but a human-made environment requiring care and maintenance. It needs to be specific to its location, its climate, its cultural and economic context. Children are not a homogenous group, and neither should their learning environments be. This is particularly the case in schools designed for children with Special Educational Needs. Emotional and psychological needs should be addressed in all schools alongside physical and sensory barriers. Technical aspects and site constraints need to be considered from the outset, acknowledging the need for non-standard solutions in terms of building envelope, accommodation, capital and operational funding. This can be complicated – but the potential rewards provide value way beyond the boundaries of the site. To achieve this outcome, including the school in the design process is crucial. School provides a taster for life. We need to get the technical recipe right.

Figure 10.13 and 10.14 Henning Larsen Architects, Frederiksbjerg School, Aarhus – Encouraging movement

CONCLUSIONS

Helen Taylor & Dr Sharon Wright

In this book we have examined UK and international examples of high-quality education spaces in our increasingly dense cities. We have looked at the role of digital technology in connecting learners in new and different ways, and explored how children and their educational experience sit within our developing urban areas. We have challenged our thinking on how schools are organised, how we build new schools, better use existing spaces and provide appropriate green spaces.

It is vital that the schools we are now building enhance and become part of the urban fabric of their cities. This requires us to collectively and strategically address a range of challenges to deliver new typologies of educational building that are fit for purpose. We need to innovate. It is unlikely that urbanisation will be reversed; countries that are developing fast are looking to those who have been managing the challenges for ideas and good practice. It could be argued that we are not doing enough to interrogate, capture and disseminate what is already working around the world.

If we truly want to deliver the best possible educational spaces, we need to move away from a fixed view of what a school is. Radical change is already evident: technology offers new opportunities and can support 24/7 learning in a variety of settings; teachers can move between classrooms so that students don't have to; buildings can be transformed from offices and shops to have a new purpose. That said, we need to further explore issues which impact upon design. Schools are not just academic factories but places where young people engage and gather a wide range of experiences that will inform and equip them for adult life. Safeguarding will always be a priority for schools, but it should not blinker us to new solutions. Ensuring that students can socialise and learn in outdoor spaces is increasingly recognised as important for their wellbeing: this should be a priority, but rarely is. When budgets are tight, we should not be delivering buildings that will be expensive to run or maintain either now or in the future.

In order to continue the debate, we feel there are several key themes around which we might focus our thinking.

CONCLUSION

(a) Educational Innovation

We have referenced examples of innovation throughout this book. The most successful examples have involved both the educators and the designers coming together to create new models. The Early Learning Village in Singapore was untested in scale and approach, yet the client bought into the design vision and worked collaboratively to ensure its success. At Notre Dame RC, the senior leaders in the school have changed how they organise year groups to accommodate being in a tall school. In Espoo, technology has allowed schooling to be dispersed in new ways. A strong educational vision, confident senior education leaders and a fully tested and understood design will give confidence to students, staff and parents. Supporting this is a clearer understanding of how young people experience our cities, and wider historical and international perspectives that shed light on the current issues our cities face. Thinking the unthinkable may be necessary if we are to make change happen, but we also need to take time and make the resources available to do this properly.

(b) Design Innovation

High Rise Schools
This remains the option perceived to have the highest risk. They need the right location and

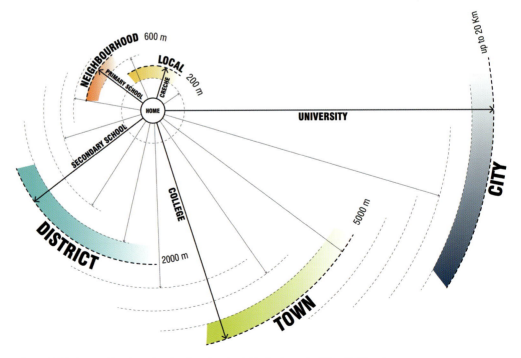

Figure 11.01 Sustainable urban planning for education (with thanks to the Urban Taskforce)

expert support to address planning, technical and construction challenges. The few high-rise schools in operation have demanded close collaboration between experienced architects and willing educators and are being watched closely. The ability to create successful educational environments for children freed from the constraints of the site footprint would solve a space challenge faced by many cities.

Mixed-use developments
It is becoming more common for schools to be embedded in new housing schemes or forming an element of wider community service provision. While this can create efficiencies and deliver great facilities for the local community, it must not be at the expense of the school's identity or curriculum delivery: the school design must be prioritised. Technical standards and pupil needs must be safeguarded throughout construction and beyond. A shared building and environment needs clear ownership of operational roles and responsibilities and an enduring means of communication between all occupants.

Adaptive reuse
There are an ever-increasing range of building types being reused for educational purposes. Repurposing existing structures can create exciting architectural outcomes as well as being a more sustainable approach. However, it is not necessarily a quicker or cheaper solution. Learning from schools that have already recycled spaces in this way will make us better at identifying opportunities for re-use and converting unconventional environments for learning. We must also leverage our digital infrastructure to broaden connections between diverse educational spaces and integrate learning into more of the urban environment.

(c) Buildability

The challenges of building should not be confused with the challenges of operating these innovative urban school environments. The former is a challenge that designers and building contractors are keen and able to resolve. Educators need more support – not because they are not able or interested, but because the expectations of student academic performance placed on them can be a significant barrier to testing diverse learning environments or new teaching methods. An innovative building needs to be partnered with innovative educational delivery and that is not always the case. And unfortunately construction costs are always a risk, whether for a new-build or remodelled environment. Schools do not have the benefit of commercial value to balance costs, and some mixed-use schemes are only viable due to local property values. High-density mixed use comes with frictions where different uses meet, whether residential and commercial, or education and transport. Managing these frictions needs a thoughtful approach that is not necessarily provided for in some procurement routes. It is only 150 years since the first skyscraper was built and the social impact of building ever taller isn't yet fully understood. For children (and adults), access to the outside and green space in cities is a fundamental human need that we are not yet prioritising.

(d) Harnessing Technology

Technology should be seen as an enabler, facilitating new ways of learning and requiring

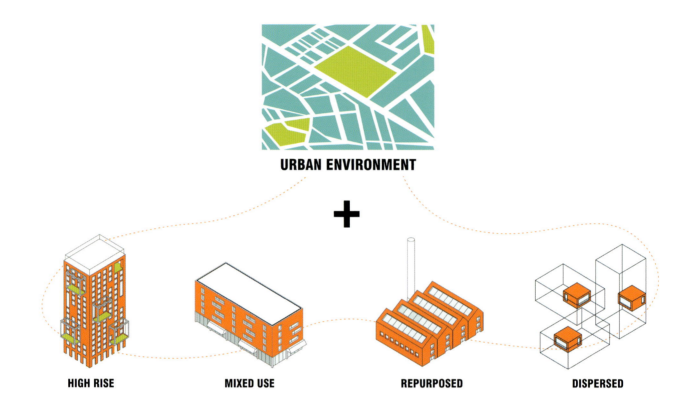

Figure 11.02 New school typologies

new thinking about how we develop appropriate spaces. As illustrated in Espoo, in cases where new digital approaches are adopted, learning can take place in a wide variety of locations, can be tailored to the needs of the individual learner, and can join up learning communities who would otherwise be isolated. Technology cannot be seen as an add-on to school design, but should be treated as a driver for change and innovation.

(e) Using the Urban Landscape

While there is general agreement about the importance of outside space for learning and social activities for young people, there is still much to do to quantify the value of good-quality space and embed this in government policymaking. This is particularly important in our urban areas where green space is at a premium and has to be made to work hard. Securing a clear brief and expertise on a project would make this a priority for all our schools, particularly those on tight sites.

CONCLUSIONS   131

We also recognise that questioning how education can be delivered to better serve communities is a subject that is relevant beyond urban environments. For example, in Scotland, Wales and Northern Ireland there are excellent examples of co-location of schools on less constrained shared sites. These approaches not only make best use of available land, they also serve a range of additional purposes. A secondary school that shares its building with a Further Education college can ensure young people receive vocational education more effectively. Small rural schools can come together to provide a wider range of specialist teaching than they could deliver individually. Bringing schools of different faiths onto one site can lead the way in creating understanding and common space for divided communities.

More research is needed on the various new models of urban schools that are being developed in the UK and internationally.

Education is dynamic and will continue to change and be influenced by its location and political context. This book does not assume that every site or existing building can accommodate repurposed building, mixed-use development or high-rise school. Rather, it challenges us to think about how we can continue to find new solutions in our towns and cities. Our educators, designers, and builders will continue to collaborate and innovate regardless of economic and political context. Our policymakers can support this important ambition by ensuring that the funding and legislative context enables these new approaches.

Not only does the school become a small city but the city becomes an exceedingly large school.[1]

Herman Hertzberger

Figure 11.03 The city as a school (overleaf)

NOTES

CHAPTER 1

1. M. Taylor, 'Latest global school climate strikes expected to beat turnout record', *Guardian*, 24 May 2019, https://www.theguardian.com/environment/2019/may/24/latest-global-school-climate-strikes-expected-to-beat-turnout-record, (accessed 28 June 2019).
2. C. Ward, *The Child in the City*, London, The Architectural Press, 1978.
3. C. Ward, C. and A. Fyson, *Streetwork: The Exploding School*, London, Routledge and Kegan Paul, 1973.
4. K. Laybourn, *Times Educational Supplement*, 2 December 1960, p xxiv; reprinted in R. Lowe, *The Death of Progressive Education: How Teachers Lost Control of the Classroom*, London, Routledge, 2007, p 46.
5. S. Woods, 'The Education Bazaar', *Harvard Educational Review*, special issue Architecture and Education, 1969, p 119.
6. R. Coles, 'Those Places They Call Schools', *Harvard Educational Review*, special issue Architecture and Education, 1969, p 55.
7. I. Illich, *Deschooling Society*, New York, Harper and Row, 1971.
8. C. Burke and I. Grosvenor, *The School I'd Like: Revisited*, 2nd edn., London, Routledge, 2015, p 61.
9. Renew Newcastle ceased operations in February 2019 following ten successful years. Its website remains active as an archive and resource. See www.renewnewcastle.org (accessed 1 July 2019).
10. Woods, p 119.
11. G. De Carlo, 'Why/How to build school buildings'. *Harvard Educational Review*, special issue Architecture and Education, 1969, p 13.

CHAPTER 2

1. United Nations Department of Economic and Social Affairs, '68% of the world population projected to live in urban areas by 2050, says UN', 16 May 2018, https://www.un.org/development/desa/en/news/population/2018-revision-of-world-urbanization-prospects.html, (accessed 16 June 2019).
2. United Nations, *The World's Cities in 2016*, Statistical Papers – United Nations (Ser. A), Population and Vital Statistics Report, New York, 2016, https://doi.org/10.18356/8519891f-en, (accessed 16 June 2019).
3. J.V. Henderson, A. Storeygard and U. Deichmann, 'Has Climate Change Driven Urbanization in Africa?', *Journal of Development Economics*, no.1, 2017, pp 60–82; UNESCO, *Global Education Monitoring Report, 2019: Migration, Displacement and Education*, Paris, 2018, https://unesdoc.unesco.org/ark:/48223/pf0000265866_eng, (accessed 16 June 2019).
4. LSE Cities, *Developing Urban Futures*, London, 2018, p 41, https://urbanage.lsecities.net/newspapers/developing-urban-futures-2018, (accessed 16 June 2019).
5. UN Habitat, *The Challenge of Slums – Global Report on Human Settlements*, revised edn., London, Earthscan Publications Ltd., 2010 (2003), Chapter 1: Development Context and the Millennium Agenda, https://unhabitat.org/wp-content/uploads/2003/07/GRHS_2003_Chapter_01_Revised_2010.pdf, (accessed 16 June 2019).
6. UNESCO, *Global Education Monitoring Report 2017/8, Summary*, Paris, 2018, https://unesdoc.unesco.org/ark:/48223/pf0000259593, (accessed 16 June 2019).

NOTES

7 UNICEF, *The State of the World's Children, 2012*, New York, 2012, pp 28–31, https://www.unicef.org/sowc2012/pdfs/SOWC-2012-Chapter-2-Childrens-rights-in-urban-settings.pdf, (accessed 16 June 2019).

8 UN Habitat, *New Urban Agenda (2016)*, p 5, http://habitat3.org/wp-content/uploads/NUA-English.pdf, (accessed 16 June 2019).

9 UN Habitat, *World Cities Report 2016*, Nairobi, 2016, p 128, http://wcr.unhabitat.org/main-report/#section_seven, (accessed 16 June 2019).

10 F. Tonkiss, *Cities by Design: The Social Life of Urban Form*, Cambridge, Polity Press, 2013, pp 111–12.

11 UNICEF, *The State of the World's Children*, pp 28–31.

12 UN Habitat, *New Urban Agenda*, pp 122–4.

13 D. Satterthwaite, 'Upgrading Dense Informal Settlements', *Urban Age Conference Papers*, London, LSE Cities, 2011.

14 'Antonio Derka School/Obranegra Arquitectos', *ArchDaily*, 28 September 2014, https://www.archdaily.com/550567/colegio-antonio-derka-santo-domingo-savio-obranegra-arquitectos, (accessed 16 June 2019).

15 A. Roy, 'Urban Informality: Towards an Epistemology of Planning', *Journal of the American Planning Association*, vol. 71, no. 2, 2005, pp 147–58; UN Habitat, *Practical Guide to Designing, Planning and Implementing Citywide Slum Upgrading Programs*, Nairobi, p 51.

16 UNICEF, *Education Uprooted: For Every Migrant, Refugee and Displaced Child, Education*, New York, 2017, p 29.

17 J. Pillay, 'Experiences of Learners from Informal Settlements', *South African Journal of Education*, vol. 24, no. 1, 2004, pp 5–9.

18 NLÉ, *Makoko Floating School, Research Report*, Amsterdam, NLE, 2012, http://www.nleworks.com/publication/makoko-research-heinrich-boll-stiftung/, (accessed 16 June 2019).

19 A. Ford, *Designing the Sustainable School*, Mulgrave, Images Publishing, 2007, pp 178–81; C. Slessor, 'Primary School, Gando, Burkina Faso: Diébédo Francis Kéré', *Architectural Review*, no. 226, 2009, pp 66–9.

20 Archdaily, 'Handmade School / Anna Heringer + Eike Roswag', *ArchDaily*, 4 March 2010, https://www.archdaily.com/51664/handmade-school-anna-heringer-eike-roswag, (accessed 16 June 2019).

CHAPTER 3

1 I. Block, 'Tokyo kindergarten by Tezuka Architects lets children run free on the roof', *Dezeen*, 2 October 2017, https://www.dezeen.com/2017/10/02/fuji-kindergarten-tokyo-tezuka-architects-oval-roof-deck-playground, (accessed 16 June 2019).

CHAPTER 4

1 Chris Jansen, correspondence with the authors.
2 Adam Patterson, correspondence with the authors.
3 Eric Sands, correspondence with the authors.

CHAPTER 5

1 Official of National Statistics, 'House Prices: How much does one square metre cost in your area?', London, 2011, https://www.ons.gov.uk/peoplepopulationandcommunity/housing/articles/housepriceshowmuchdoesonesquaremetrecostinyourarea/2017-10-11, (accessed 16 June 2019).

CHAPTER 6

1 A.C. Doyle, 'The Adventure of the Naval Treaty' in *The Memoirs of Sherlock Holmes*, London, Harmondsworth, 1950 (1893), p 215.

2 'The Tallest Academic Buildings in the World', https://www.worldatlas.com/articles/the-tallest-educational-buildings-in-the-world.html, (accessed 16 June 2019).

3 *Bromley Times*, 20 February 2019, https://www.bromleytimes.co.uk/news/plan-for-10-storey-school-in-bromley-refused-1-5898048, (accessed 16 June 2019).

CHAPTER 7

1. *Refresh, Refurbish, Remodel, Reuse*, London and Northampton, Atkins, 2001, http://www.atkinsglobal.co.uk/~/media/Files/A/Atkins-Corporate/middle-east/sectors-documents/education/library-docs/atkins-education-refurb-remodel-reuse-jan-2011.pdf, (accessed 16 June 2019).
2. Michael E. Hall of AIA, quoted in D. Barista, '8 Tips for Converting Remnant Buildings Into Schools', *Building Design and Construction*, 1 June 2007, https://www.bdcnetwork.com/8-tips-converting-remnant-buildings-schools, (accessed 16 June 2019).
3. Dr Kaisa Nuikkinen, correspondence with author.
4. Odd Eiken in *The Kunskapsskolan ('the knowledge school'): A Personalised Approach to Education*, Paris, OECD, 2011, https://www.oecd-ilibrary.org/docserver/5kgdzvmzjblv-en.pdf?expires=1560723580&id=id&accname=guest&checksum=8643CCF4E29BDB12CD311EE7110DF834, (accessed 5 July 2019).
5. *Ibid.*
6. Eden Girls' School website, 'Eden Girls' Slough New Building', 9 October 2017, https://www.edengirlsslough.com/news-story/eden-girls-slough-new-building/, (accessed 5 July 2019).
7. Scottish Government and Convention of Scottish Local Authorities (COSLA), *The Place Principle*, Edinburgh, 2019, https://www.gov.scot/publications/place-principle-introduction, (accessed 16 June 2019).

CHAPTER 8

1. See http://izonenyc.org/initiatives/school-of-one, (accessed 16 June 2019).
2. 'UK Digital Strategy', UK Government, 2017, https://www.gov.uk/government/publications/uk-digital-strategy/summary-and-annex, (accessed 16 June 2019).
3. 'Building digital capability', Jisc, https://www.jisc.ac.uk/building-digital-capability, (accessed 16 June 2019).
4. Sir Mark Grundy, correspondence with the author.
5. E. Palmer et al., 'Overcoming barriers to student engagement with Active Blending Learning: Interim Report', University of Northampton, 2017, https://www.northampton.ac.uk/ilt/wp-content/uploads/sites/2/2017/10/Student-Engagement-with-ABL-Interim-Report-v3-October-2017.pdf, (accessed 16 June 2019).
6. 'A new building to "spark" the imagination', Southampton Solent University, 27 July 2016, https://www.solent.ac.uk/news/life-at-solent/2016/a-new-building-to-spark-the-imagination, (accessed 16 June 2019).

CHAPTER 9

1. 'Children's visits to natural environments: new evidence', Natural England, 2015, https://www.gov.uk/government/news/childrens-visits-to-natural-environments-new-evidence, (accessed 16 June 2019).
2. R. Louv, *Last Child in the Woods: Saving Our Children from Nature-deficit Disorder*, revised edn., London, Atlantic Books, 2008 (2005).
3. 'It's official – spending time outside is good for you', *Science Daily*, 6 July 2018, https://www.sciencedaily.com/releases/2018/07/180706102842.htm, (accessed 16 June 2019).
4. P. Dadvand, et al., 'Green spaces and cognitive development in primary schoolchildren', *Proceedings of the Natural Academy of Sciences of the United States of America*, 2015, https://www.pnas.org/content/112/26/7937, (accessed 16 June 2019).
5. N.M. Wells, 'At Home With Nature: Effects of "Greenness" on Children's Cognitive Functioning', *Environment and Behavior*, vol. 32, no. 6, November 2000, pp 775–95; H.L. Burdette and R.C. Whitaker, 'Resurrecting Free Play in Young Children Looking Beyond Fitness and Fatness to Attention, Affiliation, and Affect', *JAMA Pediatrics*, vol 159, no. 1, January 2005, pp 46–50, https://jamanetwork.com/journals/jamapediatrics/fullarticle/485902, (accessed 16 June 2019).
6. E. Reed, *The Necessity of Experience*, New Haven and London, Yale University Press, 1996.
7. R.M. Milteer, et al., 'The Importance of Play in Promoting Healthy Child Development and Maintaining Strong Parent-Child Bonds', *Pediatrics*, vol. 129,

no. 1, pp 2014–13, January 2012, https://pediatrics.aappublications.org/content/129/1/e204, (accessed 16 June 2019).

8   A.F. Taylor et al., 'Views of Nature and Self-Discipline: Evidence from Inner City Children', *Journal of Environmental Psychology*, vol. 22, no. 1, March 2002, pp 49–63, https://www.researchgate.net/publication/222546487_Views_of_Nature_and_Self-Discipline_Evidence_from_Inner_City_Children, (accessed 16 June 2019).

9   F.E. Kuo and A.F. Taylor, 'A Potential Natural Treatment for Attention-Deficit/Hyperactivity Disorder: Evidence From a National Study', *American Journal of Public Health*, vol. 94, no. 9, September 2004, pp 1580–6, https://www.ncbi.nlm.nih.gov/pmc/articles/PMC1448497, (accessed 16 June 2019) A.F. Taylor et al., 'Coping with ADD: The Surprising Connection to Green Play Settings', *Environment and Behavior*, vol. 33, no. 1, pp 54–77, January 2001.

10 Louv, 2008.

11 A.F. Taylor and F.E. Kuo, 'Children with attention deficits concentrate better after walk in the park, *Journal of Attention Disorders*, vol. 12, no. 5, pp 402–9, March 2009, https://www.ncbi.nlm.nih.gov/pubmed/18725656, (accessed 16 June 2019).

12 Dongying Li and W.C. Sullivan, 'Impact of views to school landscapes on recovery from stress and mental fatigue', *Landscape and Urban Planning*, vol. 148, April 2016, pp 149–58.

13 N.M. Wells and G.W. Evans, 'Nearby Nature: A Buffer of Life Stress among Rural Children', *Environment and Behavior*, vol. 35, no. 3, May 2003, pp 311–30, https://pdfs.semanticscholar.org/f1b3/b8b51f9b11295debee2b9b4956e24422e6f9.pdf, (accessed 16 June 2019).

14 C. Kelz et al., 'The Restorative Effects of Redesigning the Schoolyard: A Multi-Methodological, Quasi-Experimental Study in Rural Austrian Middle Schools', *Environment and Behavior*, vol. 47, no. 2, January 2013.

15 K.E. Lee et al., '40-second green roof views sustain attention: The role of micro-breaks in attention restoration' *Journal of Environmental Psychology*, vol. 42, June 2015, pp 182–9.

16 Laura Donnelly, 'Tripling in children suffering Vitamin D deficiency', *Telegraph*, 21 October 2014, https://www.telegraph.co.uk/journalists/laura-donnelly/11175544/Tripling-in-children-suffering-Vitamin-D-deficiency.html, (accessed 16 June 2019).

17 For principles of biophilic design, see https://www.designingbuildings.co.uk/wiki/Biophilic_design, (accessed 16 June 2019).

18 'Street Tree Cost benefit Analysis', GreenBlue Urban, https://www.greenblue.com/gb/resource-centre/street-tree-cost-benefit-analysis.

19 E.G. McPherson et al., 'Chicago's Urban Forest Ecosystem: Results of the Chicago Urban Forest Climate Project', United States Department of Agriculture, January 1994.

20 as item 18 above.

21 'Your Partner For A Greener Future', ANS Group Global, 2018, https://www.ansgroupglobal.com/sites/default/files/fields/downloads/files/ANS_Global_Brochure_2018_Download.pdf, (accessed 16 June 2019).

22 K. Callison, 'Multigenerational Play', Playground Professionals, 19 March 2018, https://www.playgroundprofessionals.com/playground/accessibility/multigenerational-play103, (accessed 16 June 2019).

23 Louv, 2008, p 9; P.H. Kahn and S.R. Kellert, *Children and Nature: Psychological, Sociocultural, and Evolutionary Investigations*, Cambridge, MA, MIT Press, 2002

24 R. and S. Kaplan, *The Experience of Nature: A Psychological Perspective*, Cambridge University Press, 1989; R. Kaplan, 'Wilderness perception and psychological benefits: An analysis of a continuing program', *Journal of Leisure Sciences*, vol. 6, no. 3, 1984, pp 271–90.

25 J. Gilbert et al., *Dirt Is Good: The Advantage of Germs for Your Child's Developing Immune System*, New York, St Martin's Press, 2017.

26 G. Paton, 'UK Sport chief: Primary pupils "unable to run or jump"', *Telegraph*, 16 January 2013, https://www.telegraph.co.uk/education/educationnews/9806772/UK-Sport-chief-Primary-pupils-unable-to-run-or-jump.html, (accessed 16 June 2019).

27 E. Haug et al., 'Physical environmental characteristics and individual interests as correlates of physical activity in Norwegian secondary schools: The health behaviour in school-aged children study' *International Journal of Behavioral Nutrition and Phsyical Activity*, vol. 5, no. 47, 2008.

28 M. Robinson, '11–18 Secondary School Play: The research behind play in school', Grounds for Learning, 2014, https://www.londonplay.org.uk/resources/0000/1737/The_value_of_play_in_11-18_secondary_schools_Jan_2015.pdf, (accessed 16 June 2019).

29 *Ibid.*

30 *Ibid.*

CHAPTER 10

1 D. Mumovic et al., 'Indoor Air Quality in London's Schools', Greater London Authority, May 2018, https://www.london.gov.uk/sites/default/files/gla_iaq_report_with_nts.pdf, accessed 16 June 2019).

2 'How pollution affects indoor air quality in buildings', *CIBSE Journal*, June 2018, https://www.cibsejournal.com/technical/learning-the-limits-how-outdoor-pollution-affects-indoor-air-quality-in-buildings, (accessed 16 June 2019).

3 Dianne Western, the Landscape Partnership, conversation with the author.

4 'Harris Westminster Sixth Form Academy', Nicholas Hare Architects, https://www.nicholashare.co.uk/projects/view/harris-westminster-sixth-form-academy, (accessed 16 June 2019).

5 School of One in New York City: An Implementation Guide. See https://www.slideshare.net/iZoneNYC/school-of-one-in-new-york-city-an-implementation-guide, (accessed 16 June 2019).

6 'Frederiksbjerg School / Henning Larsen Architects + GGP Architects', *Archdaily*, 16 November 2016, https://www.archdaily.com/799521/frederiksbjerg-school-henning-larsen-architects-plus-gpp-architects, (accessed 16 June 2019).

7 'A School in Motion in Aarhus', *Detail*, September 2018, p 72, http://dl.booktolearn.com/emagazines2/architecture/Detail_September_2018.pdf, (accessed 16 June 2019).

CONCLUSION

1 Herman Hertzberger, *Space and Learning* https://www.amazon.co.uk/Herman-Hertzberger-Learning-students-architecture/dp/9064506442 (accessed 16 June 2019).

INDEX

Note: page numbers in italics refer to illustrations and figures.

absenteeism 14
Academy schools 21–2, 44
access to education 13–14, 15–16
ADP Architects 73
air quality 50, 98–9, 115
All Age Schools 29–31
Alsop Architects 111
ANS Global 98
Antonio Derka School, Colombia 19
arrival and departure 22, 34, 36, 50
atria 64, 66

Belham Primary School, Southwark 26, *107*, 114
blended learning 6
Bobby Moore Academy, Stratford, London 66–8
Bogle Architects *34–40*
Bonetti/Kozerski *58*
BREEAM 106, 107
building design and construction 113–23
building reuse 71–83, 129
Burkina Faso, Lycée Schorge Secondary School 16–17

Cardinal Pole Catholic School, Hackney *27*
Chandigarh, Sector 23 Higher Secondary School *97*
circulation 23, 24, 27, 35–6, 62–3
city as school 1–4

collaborative learning 8, 52, 74, 75, 86
co-location 131
community facilities 43–6
Community Infrastructure Levy (CIL) 46
'community of learners' 21
computer-based learning *see* digital technology
conversions 71–83
Cottrell & Vermeulen *23–4*

David Morley Architects *54*, *109*, *111*
daylighting 53, 61, 66, 68, 72, 96
Deer Park School, Richmond 47, *47*
'deschooling' 3
digital city 89–91
digital technology 4–6, 7, 8–9, 124, 129–30
distributed school 6–9
Dixon Jones Architects *105–6*
drop-off points 22, 34, 36, 50
Dulwich Hamlet Junior School 95

Early Learning Village (ELV), Singapore 33–41, *128*
early years 22, 25
Eaton House School, London *98*
Eden Girls' School, Slough 73, 80
Education and Skills Funding Agency (ESFA) 46
education technology (EdTech) 85–91
entrance 50

Esa Ruskeepää Architects *90*
external spaces *see* outdoor space

Faraday School, Southwark *111*
Farrer Huxley Associates *100*
FCBStudios *44–5, 51–2*
'flipped classroom' *6*
Floating School, Nigeria *16–17*
Frank Barnes School for Deaf Children *54, 109, 111*
Frederiksbjerg School, Aarhus *124*
Fuji Kindergarten *25, 99*
funding *46–8*

Global South *11*
global urbanisation *11–13*
green space *93–111*
green walls *98*

Harris Aspire Academy, South Norwood *74*
Harris Invictus Academy, Croydon *117–19*
Harris Westminster Sixth Form Academy *80, 81, 123*
Haverstock Associates *26, 28–9, 107, 114*
Hazel Wolf K-8 E-STEM School, Seattle *98*
Henning Larsen Architects *125*
Heringer, Anna *18*
HGO (Heimdalsgades Overbygningsskole), Copenhagen, *77*
high streets *5–6*
Highland Academy Charter School, Anchorage, Alaska *78, 123*
high-rise schools *22, 57–69, 128–9*
Holy Trinity Primary School, Dalston *48, 49*

internal 'streets' *27, 66–7*
international development goals *13*

Jane Drew Architect *97*
Jestico + Whiles *27*

Katy Staton Landscape Architecture *109*
Kéré Architecture *17*
Kier Construction *47*
Kings Cross Academy *54, 109, 111*
Kunskapsskolan ('Knowledge School') *75*

Lagos, Floating School *16–17*
land acquisition *46*
Landscape Partnership *101, 111*
landscaping *95–9, 101, 102, 104–7*
Landskrona Charter School, Sweden *75, 124*
Livity School, Streatham *28–9*
LocatED *48*

Macgregor Smith Landscape Architects *105–6*
Makoko Floating School *16–17*
Marlborough Primary School, London *105, 106*
METI (Modern Education and Training Institute), Bangladesh *18–19*
mixed use developments *43–55, 78, 129*
movement *see* circulation

NAC Architecture *98*
natural areas *see* green space
Nicholas Hare Architects *81–2, 100*
NLÉ *16*
Notre Dame School, London *23–4, 128*

Obranegra Arquitectos *19*
Opinmäki Learning Centre, Espoo *90–1, 128, 130*
outdoor space *25, 26, 29, 36–7, 48, 52, 53, 68, 93–111, 124*
out-of school rate *14*

overlooking 53
overshadowing 53

Paris Oasis Schools Project *108*
Penoyre & Prasad *67–8*
Perkins + Will Architects *64–6*, *116*, *121*
Perkins Eastman Architects *58*
planning agreements *46*
play space *28*, *36*, *37*, *49*, *52*, *93*, *99–102*, *103–4*, *115*
Plymouth School of Creative Arts (PSCA) *44*
primary *26*, *48*, *50*, *100*
Prior Weston Primary School, London *100*
PTE Architects *79*

Regent High School, London *27*
repurposing *71–83*, *123*, *129*
RIBA Plan of Work *113–23*
Robert Browning Primary School *115*
Rock Townsend Architects *48–9*
roof gardens *96*
rooftop spaces *24*, *26*, *48*, *52*, *100*, *100–1*, *105*, *115*, *122*
Rosan Bosch Studio *76*
Royal Greenwich Trust School *101*, *102*, *120*

School of One *86*, *87*
Scotland *79*, *110*
Scott Brownrigg *60–3*, *117–19*
secondary *26–7*
Section 106 (S106) agreements *46*
shared facilities *43–6*

SHaW Futures Academy, Bromley, London *60–3*
slums *12–13*, *15*
Special Educational Needs (SEN) *22*, *28–9*, *104*
sports facilities *52*, *66*, *67*, *74*, *101*
St Benedict School, Ealing *30*
St Mary's RC Primary School, Battersea *45*, *50*, *51*
Strömberg School, Helsinki *77*

tall schools *22*, *57–69*, *128–9*
Teach to One, New York *85*, *124*
Tezuka Architects *25*, *99*
Tidemill Academy, Deptford *78*, *79*
travel to school *7*, *50*, *116*
trees *96*, *98–9*, *107*
Trinity School, Sevenoaks, Kent *80*

urban planning *14–15*
urbanisation *11–13*
UTC@Harbourside, Newhaven, Sussex *77*

Van Heyningen and Haward *30*
Vignoles Gymnasium, Paris *96*
Vittra Telefonplan, Stockholm *75–6*

Walters and Cohen Architects *27*, *101–2*
West College Scotland *79*
William Jones College, Chicago *64–5*, *69*, *116*, *121*
World School, New York City *58*
Wynne-Williams Associates *95*, *115*

PICTURE CREDITS

ADP / Andrew Heptinstall Figure 7.02

Alan Williams Photography / Nicholas Hare Figures 7.00, 7.07

ANS Global Figure 9.05

Architectural Press Archive / RIBA Collections Figure 9.01

Benjamin Staehli Figure 2.05

Bogle Architects Figures 4.01, 4.02, 4.04

Claire James, Campaign against Climate Change Figure 1.04

City of Espoo Figure 8.05

D'Arcy Norman from Calgary, Canada Figure 0.01

Dan Hill Figure 1.06

David Morley Architects Figure 5.08

Dennis Gilbert Figures 3.08–10

Dennis Gilbert / VIEW Pictures Figures 3.07, 6.11, 6.13–14

Dianne Western Figures 9.16, 9.17

Dusty Gedge Figure 9.03

FCB Studios Figures 5.02, 5.06-07

Galliford Try / Pollard Thomas Edwards Architects Figure 7.06

Galliford Try / Scott Brownrigg Figure 10.05

Haverstock Figure 10.01

Hufton & Crow Figures 5.0–01, 10.13, 11.00

Hundven-Clements Photography Figures 0.00, 10.06, 10.08, 10.09

Infinitude / Bogle Architects Figures 4.00, 4.03, 4.05, 4.06

James R. Steinkamp Figures 2.00, 6.00, 6.07, 6.09–10, 10.00, 10.03, 10.11

Joakim Formo Figure 1.05

John Waldron / spaces4learning Figure 7.05

John Sturrock Photographer Figure 9.15

Juliet Davis / redrawn from Unesco Institute for Statistics Figure 2.02

Kéré Architecture Figure 2.04

Kim Wendt Figure 7.04

Laurent Bourgogne / Ville de Paris Figure 9.14

Lidl Great Britain / Boyes Rees Architects Ltd Figure 5.03

PICTURE CREDITS

Liz Finlayson Figure 8.04

Luca Pioltelli Figures 6.01–02

MATT+FIONA / Patrick Mateer Figure 1.03

Matt Clayton Photography Figures 5.04, 5.05

MBB Architects / Frank Oudeman Figure 9.00

Michael Buchanan Figures 7.03, 10.12

NAC Architecture / Benjamin Benschneider Figure 9.06

Nicholas Hare Architects Figure 7.08

NLÉ Figure 2.03

Obranegra Arquitectos / Luis Adriano Ramirez Figure 2.06

Paul Riddle Figures 9.11–12

Penoyre & Prasad Figure 6.12

Perkins & Will Figure 6.08

Peter Cook Figure 3.06

Peter Durant Figures 1.00, 9.08

Portsmouth College Figure 8.00

Rachel Hain Figure 1.02

RIBA Collections Figure 9.04

RIBA Schools Programme Figures 1.07, 8.03

Scott Brownrigg Figures 2.01, 6.05, 6.06, 10.04, 10.07, 11.01–03

Scott Brownrigg / redrawn from School of One in New York City: An Implementation Guide Figures 8.01–02

Simon Kennedy Photography Figure 3.05, 9.13

Tezuka Architects Figures 3.04, 9.07

The Landscape Partnership Figures 9.09 and 9.10

Tim Griffith Figure 7.01

Tom Cronin Figures 3.00–03

Tony Ray-Jones / RIBA Collections Figure 1.01

van Heyningen & Haward Architects Figure 3.11

Virklund Sport Figure 10.14

Walters & Cohen Figure 10.10

Wates Construction Figures 6.03, 6.04

Wynne Williams Associates Figure 9.02, 10.02